THE DEAR WALTER PAPERS

SOME RAVE REVIEWS FROM FAMOUS PEOPLE

Walter Sisulu: "Nelson who?"

The South African Foreign Minister: "Nzzzzzzz ..."
(© A Nzo)

Henry Kissinger: "South Africa will have to learn to live
with this book."

Robert Mugabe: "Some of my best friends are men."

© David Beresford 1997
The moral right of the author has been asserted.

First published in 1997 by
Mail & Guardian
PO Box 32362
Braamfontein
2017
South Africa

ISBN 0 620 21163 6

Typesetting, reproduction, and cover by Mail & Guardian
Cover cartoon by Derek Bauer
Printed and bound by Creda Press

A
MAIL&GUARDIAN
BOOK

THE

Dear Walter

PAPERS

&

A NOTE FROM THE PUBLISHERS

Certain critics who have called into question the authenticity of the priceless Dear Walter Papers have cited, in support of their case, an early denial by Mr Walter Sisulu (Retired) that he had received any such letters from the President. We have, however, discovered in our archives the following letter which throws new light on what was obviously a premature denial.

December 18 1995

Dear Nelson,

I write to you in a great hurry and with much regret to tell of a terrible misfortune. Returning home recently from the Push-a-Bottle-Top Challenge Cup for Veterans at the Orlando community hall, I happened to see the postman struggling to push what appeared to be several envelopes into a drainpipe. I stopped to give him a hand and after much shoving, kicking and cursing we managed to get the material inside. Shaking hands in mutual congratulation I inquired, conversationally, as to why he was pushing letters into drainpipes. "That," he said importantly, nodding towards the drain, "is the future; it's the information superhighway." Striding off purposefully in the direction of the next drainpipe he added, over his shoulder: "It was old man Sisulu's mail."

A trifle upset at this description of myself — I had, after all, only just been pipped to fifth position in the Challenge Cup and would no doubt have done better if Mrs Khumalo had not stepped on my bottle-top — I went inside to recover from the afternoon's exertions. I was in the process of devouring one of Ma Adelaide's chocolate biscuits, washed down with a cup of cocoa, my mind wandering around the great issues of the day — Who created the universe and did he need a mortgage? Why is now, now and what happened to yesterday? Why does Major Gregory exist? — when suddenly I was hit by a thought. Rushing outside and examining my letter box from every possible angle, it was confirmed: there was no link between it and the drain-pipe. I did not appear to have been connected to the information superhighway!!

To cut a long story short, after various telephone calls to Pallo Jordan's office and inspections *in loco* by computer experts and teams of plumbers, I was finally presented with a soggy mush which, it tran-spired, was my mail for the last year, inadvertently lost in cyberspace. Over the last couple of nights Ma Adelaide and I, with the help of huge quantities of chocolate biscuits and cocoa, have been painstak-ingly piecing it together. And of course we have discovered — amidst such items as appeals from the World Wildlife Fund to save an endangered species and adopt FW de Klerk — your wonderful, trag-ic, joyous and above all courageous letters.

"How did he survive such desperate times?" is the question Ma and I kept murmuring to one another as we pored breathlessly over them. What next in the extraordinary saga that is the history of our beloved country? What more can happen to those larger-than-life fig-ures which flicker so briefly across these pages of time? Will the mys-terious disappearance of Richard Steyn ever be explained, or has the Irish desperado, O'Reilly, disposed of the body in a vat of tomato sauce? Will your guru, Peter "Hawking" O'Sullivan, solve the central riddle of the universe he has set himself and establish once and for all whether there is life after Mandela? Will you ever succeed in delivering the divorce papers and at what horrendous cost in terms of human lives? What happened to the Second Coming of Castro and will American ambassador Princeton Lyman succeed this time around in having him defoliated? Will Alfred Nzo ever wake up again? Can Tokyo Sexwale's aunt's dachshund, Wors, kick the cocaine habit and survive the increasingly desperate attempts by the drug barons to kid-nap him? When will Robert Mugabe emerge from the closet and what will he be wearing?

It is a correspondence which I shall long treasure and which, I am sure, will go down as one of the great contributions to contemporary history, not to mention literature; a graphic account of the momentous events through which we have been living and through which we will continue to live. God help us all.

How saddened I am that I did not have the opportunity to offer you succour when you were living through those crises, old friend. But rest assured I will stand by you in the New Year, when both Adelaide and I will be eagerly awaiting the postman's knock. Just try and remember to put a postage stamp on next time. Otherwise it plays hell with the drainage system.

Your comrade,
Walter

1994

On May 10 1994 Nelson Mandela was inaugurated as President of a democratic South Africa at a ceremony attended by world leaders ranging from Fidel Castro to American Vice-President Al Gore and Palestine's Yassar Arafat. Mandela's daughter Zeni acted as "first lady", resplendent in a top hat of startling dimensions. Walter Sisulu was the first guest of honour to take his seat on the podium.

Security force commanders — many under investigation at the time by the Goldstone commission of inquiry into political violence — also attended in a display of loyalty which few took seriously. The event, witnessed by the world, passed off peacefully. But, some time after publication of the following letter, it was reported that there had indeed been a right-wing plot to blow up Mandela and the podium.

Eugene Terre'Blanche was leader of the neo-Nazi Afrikaner Weerstandsbeweging (AWB, or Afrikaner Resistance Movement) and was renowned for wearing green underpants. A theory has been floated that he was an out-of-work clown "planted" on the AWB by the National Intelligence Service to make a laughing stock of the right-wing cause. On one occasion he made an effort to sleep with his horse in the apparent belief that it was the practice among warrior peoples of the past, but moved into the local Holiday Inn after discovering the beast snored.

After the inauguration Mandela faced the task of choosing his first Cabinet. Cyril Ramaphosa, a keen fly-fisherman, is believed to have been offered Foreign Affairs, but turned it down in pique at being given a subordinate position to Thabo Mbeki, appointed Deputy President.

Sol Kerzner is a controversial casino boss who used to boast a friendship with Mbeki. "Jomo", who features prominently in the Dear Walter Papers, was personal bodyguard to Mandela.

African National Congress ministers had to re-stock their offices when it was discovered their National Party predecessors had taken most of the furniture and equipment on their departure.

Pik Botha, then the longest-serving Foreign Minister in the world, was reported to be particularly distraught at his loss of office.

Office of the President

May 15 1994

Dear Walter,

So we made it. Who would have guessed, in those far off days of the Rivonia trial when Percy Yutar was drooling over our death warrants, that it would come to this: the great and the good from around the planet gathered to watch the Chief Justice swear me in as head of state to the salutes of security force commanders. How good it was to have you there for the occasion. Sorry they gave you the wrong time; it must have been cold on the podium, but at least you saw the dawn break on the new South Africa.

You ask about Zeni's hat. Well, don't tell anyone, but it was Basie Smit. You know: the police general that judge — Goldstone — keeps gabbling about? He came to us a few hours before the inauguration to warn us that his Intelligence Department had uncovered a plot by the AWB to fly a small aeroplane filled with explosives into the podium. He said they had it all under control; they had put an explosive device on board the plane and they were going to blow it up once it was in the air. But they needed some kind of radar device near to me all the time, just to make sure. So they had built it into this huge hat and they wanted Zeni to wear it.

She was a bit reluctant at first, protesting it made her look like something out of the Mad Hatter's tea party. But ever since she became a Swazi princess she has tried to be gracious, so she agreed to wear it. Basie Smit, who handled it very gingerly, would not let us look inside; he said the equipment was "top secret". It was a terrible weight on her head, which is why she had that frozen look on her face.

As it transpired it was all for nothing. Basie told us afterwards that the AWB voted unanimously for Eugene Terre'Blanche to fly the plane, but he cried off at the last minute; he said he had a sore back after sleeping the night before with his horse. The funny thing was that Basie did not know about the cancellation of the plot at the time. Jomo says he saw him behind a stone wall at the back of the Union Buildings, sweat pouring down his face as he pumped frantically at one of those plungers they use to set off dynamite blasts — presumably under the misapprehension Terre'Blanche had taken off. We did not tell him we had seen him. You know how it is with these generals, you have to let them save face. But it is nice to see him go to so much trouble to protect me — it just shows how wrong people can be.

Immediately after the inauguration we had to get to work choosing a Cabinet. That led to much squabbling, Thabo and Cyril shouting at each other about fly-fishing with the bosses and Sol Kerzner and BMWs and penthouses! Heaven knows what it all had to do with the job of Deputy President. Winnie insisted on giving it to Thabo in the end.

You will see that Winnie is Deputy Minister of Arts and Culture and Science and Technology. Naidoo got Reconstruction and Development after making a fiery speech about the need to wage class war on swimming pools. Gatsha insisted on Home Affairs; he said it had been such fun organising the KwaZulu-Natal election and he wanted to do the whole country next time. We had a terrible time waking Nzo up, to find out if he wanted Foreign Affairs.

Finally we moved into the Union Buildings, although that was not without a fuss either. De Klerk had pinched all the light bulbs, ashtrays and headed notepaper. We discovered Pik Botha hiding behind the curtains in the Foreign Affairs offices. He started crying when Jomo led him to the door and eventually agreed to go if he could make one last call from his red telephone. It was to Atomic Energy headquarters and when they answered he started babbling: "Armageddon is here, press the button, press the button ..." No one had the heart to remind him that all the bombs had been melted down.

So here I am, sitting at the seat of power. Just between you and me, Walter, I wish we were back in the lime quarry. As I write this I can see Winnie out the window, coming up the stairs with a mortarboard on her head and two cans of paint in her hands. She has painted the statue of General Louis Botha and his horse blue and yellow. Some idiot has told her about Van Gogh.

Yours from the top,
Nelson

Early days of the Mandela presidency were marked by attempts to find some way of dealing with Chief Mangosuthu "Gatsha" Buthelezi. He was appointed to the powerful Cabinet post of Home Affairs on the principle that "it is better to have him in the tent throwing assegais out than outside the tent throwing assegais in" (there are vulgar variations on this ancient Zulu proverb). Attempts were also made by the ANC to drive a wedge between the Zulu monarch, King Goodwill Zwelithini, and the chief — his uncle — in the hope it would rob Buthelezi of his tribal influence.

In the dying days of apartheid rule President FW de Klerk gave a huge tract of tribal land — amounting to roughly a quarter of the province of KwaZulu-Natal — to the King in an apparent attempt to shore up Inkatha control of the region when the ANC came to power.

Buthelezi, who is a passionate public speaker, has earned a place for himself in the Guinness Book of Records by delivering the world's longest speech. His feat, in addressing the KwaZulu legislative assembly for 11 days, totally eclipsed the previous record of 46 hours and 10 minutes set by university students in Dublin. The students set their record as a Rag stunt. Buthelezi was not engaged in a Rag stunt. He is reported to have caused consternation among KwaZulu parliamentarians by telling them, on the fifth day of his address: "That concludes my opening remarks ..."

OFFICE OF THE PRESIDENT

May 27 1994

Dear Walter,

Life is of course very busy for me. No sooner was the excitement of the inauguration over than we had to face the first parliamentary session. My biggest complaint is I don't have much time to think.

I used to do much of my thinking in the early morning pedalling my exercise bicycle. But it has become a bit difficult with all the noise Jomo makes. Ever since he went on a Secret Service course in

Washington he insists on going everywhere with me. He has fixed
one of those toy car dashboards to the back of my exercise bike —
you know, with one of those make-believe steering wheels? It isn't
the gear changes I mind so much, but the siren noises he makes.

We had some slight difficulty, as you might have read, with
KwaZulu-Natal. You know our people down there won't accept the
election result. Jacob Zuma keeps going on about Eshowe, where
800% of the population voted. On top of it all came these allegations that De Klerk gave the province to King Zwelithini as a
farewell present before the elections. I asked Chief Buthelezi about
it and he demanded to know what was wrong with the King having a
bit of land and when his great-great-grandfather Shaka ... well, you
know what it's like with the chief, Walter; one just switches off after
a while.

I'm having some difficulty in getting the chief to come to Cape
Town. He was meant to be here on Friday, but he had arranged
some sort of ceremony to introduce the King to the new KwaZulu-
Natal Cabinet. Apparently the King failed to turn up and it all
became very embarrassing. The chief insisted on going ahead with
his prepared speech and the opening lines were: "I will not allow
any leader, any political party, or any force to prise me away from
your elbow, Your Majesty. I will be there constantly at your side
whatever happens." There was a lot of sniggering among the
courtiers, I believe.

It is difficult to stop Gatsha as you probably know. I'm told he
insists on reading these speeches of his — memorandums he calls
them — whenever he meets a foreign leader. He once delivered one
at Versailles and the paramedics had to be called in to give mouth-
to-mouth resuscitation to Mitterrand who fell asleep with his face in
the vichyssoise.

There was a terrible panic at the beginning of Monday's Cabinet
meeting when it was thought that he was pulling a memorandum out
of his pocket, but it was only his handkerchief — I don't suppose
the sight of a man blowing his nose has ever been met with such
relief. As it was we made a late start. Nzo had to be carried in, in
his armchair; Foreign Affairs is very keen that we should not dis-
turb his sleep too much, because they need him awake for the pre-

sentation of new ambassadors. Winnie caused further delays because she insisted on having what she called a national art treasure hung on the wall of the Cabinet room. It is a nude study of her, in the style of Titian apparently, lying on what looks like a psychiatrist's couch under a tree with a frangipani clenched in her teeth and an apple falling on her head. I did not have the heart to object; she is taking her Arts and Science portfolios very seriously. But she has hung it behind where Thabo sits, at the bottom end of the table, and whenever I look up she is leering down at me. It makes it difficult to think.

Yours,
Nelson

The first visit to liberated South Africa by a French head of state was marred by in-fighting between officials responsible for protocol, the French proving anxious that President Mandela show respect for President Mitterrand.

The early months of coalition government in South Africa were marked by rivalry between the two Deputy Presidents, Thabo Mbeki and FW de Klerk. Although there was no provision in the Constitution for a distinction between the two posts, Mbeki insisted that — as a member of the majority party — he was Senior Deputy President.

Red mercury is a fabled substance which is said to be a vital ingredient for the manufacture of miniature nuclear bombs of such dimensions they can be concealed in ball-point pens. It is much prized among investigative reporters at the Johannesburg Star.

OFFICE OF THE PRESIDENT

July 8 1994

Dear Walter,

I have just survived the French. The experience has given me a fresh understanding of the Napoleonic Wars.

When President Mitterrand announced he was coming I assumed it would be enough to push the parsley and a few frog's legs his way — even if it did mean declaring the SPCA an unrest area. But his advance team had a list of demands the size of the Encyclopaedia Britannica. I had to be at the airport half an hour early to make sure I was in time to carry his bags. They were very disappointed to discover there was no wall between Johannesburg and Soweto; it appears he was planning to climb on top of it and shout "*Je suis un* Sowetan". And there was a stand-up row with Frene Ginwala over whether they could install giant fans in Parliament, to underline pointed references he was planning to make to the winds of change.

We arranged for him to switch on the new electricity grid in Khayelitsha. Winnie had borrowed the state Mercedes, so I had to hitch-hike. Mitterrand arrived in a cavalcade made up of 13 cars, 26 motorcycle out-riders, three tanks and two helicopters. It was quite impressive, but the effect was ruined when he got out of his stretch Citroën and Johnson Ngxobongwana, who was meant to greet him, was heard to ask General Meiring: "Who's the midget?"

It turned out there was no electricity available in Khayelitsha, but experts from Eskom-Electricité de France — the joint consortium which has built the grid — had managed to rig up a light-bulb on top of a pole for him to switch on. Unfortunately the battery turned out to be flat, so we had to send Basie Smit up to put a candle on top while we all cheered. I don't know what the good people of Khayelitsha thought of it all.

But the visit ended up a success. Mitterrand was particularly pleased when I presented him with a medal — the Highest and Most Meritorious Order of Good Hope, Category A, Class 1: Grandest Cross of the First Degree with Spangles (Gold with Money Back Guarantee) — particularly when we pointed out that he was the only foreigner ever to have received it. Actually Jomo made it. I just hope Mitterrand does not suck on it, because he's liable to get lead poisoning.

I used to think the work of a president was a matter of making a few simple decisions — you know, declarations of war and so forth — with a couple of gracious speeches thrown in. But I am more like a personnel manager, spending my time soothing egos.

Take FW and Thabo. There's been tension between them ever since they became Deputy Presidents — endless squabbling over who is the more important. It started with Thabo signing himself "First Deputy President" in his official correspondence. FW then started calling himself the "Premier Deputy President". Thabo started referring to FW as the "Baldest Deputy President". Since then it's been downhill.

I cannot allow them to be present at the same state functions; they are liable to start wrestling over the chair to my right, or trample a VIP flat in the rush to be first to shake his or her hand. There have been break-ins at both their offices in the middle of the night; Mike Louw says it is their aides, sent in to measure the size of each other's desks.

FW rushed off to London last week and got himself a seat in the

Royal Box at Wimbledon; sitting there with a diadem on his head, giving the thumbs-down every time Navratilova double-faulted and borrowing Princess Di's cordless telephone to make "wish-you-were-here" calls to Thabo.

Thabo was in a terrible state. I heard him on the telephone, shouting at the White House that they would not get another ounce of red mercury for their bombs if he wasn't allowed to referee the World Cup Final.

Stay warm, old colleague,

Yours as ever

Nelson

In July 1994 Mandela underwent a cataract operation. The surgeon, Dr Percy Amoils, confided to the press afterwards that the head of state was also suffering from "kerato conjunctivitis sicca" — his tear-glands having been burned out by the alkaline nature of the limestone on Robben Island.

Joe Nhlanhla, the South African intelligence chief, is a mysterious figure who is rarely heard in public. On occasion he has been mistaken for the President's chauffeur.

Michael Heseltine, an unsuccessful candidate for the British premiership, is known as "Tarzan" because of his sometimes apelike antics in the House of Commons.

OFFICE OF THE PRESIDENT

July 22 1994

Dear Walter,

I'm just out of hospital after an eye operation. It was quite an ordeal. I had been looking forward to a rest from the cares of office, but I didn't have much of that, thanks to my surgeon. The man could not stop talking. I told him about the limestone syndrome we all suffer after our time on the Island and he got very excited, saying that this was going to make him world famous. He babbled on about articles he was going to write for the American and British medical journals, about "The Man Who Couldn't Cry". The only respite I got was when journalists telephoned in and he rushed off to babble to them.

Frankly I came close to tears despite the lime damage, what with his incessant chatter — and then Winnie. I had left strict instructions that she was not allowed in to the clinic. She was to be told I was still recovering from the anaesthetic. You can imagine that was not much of a bar to Winnie. I had her trying to break in through the fan light and banging on my window shouting: "Nelson — I've come to nurse you." It was enough to make a grown man cry; get mixed up in playing doctors and nurses with

21

Winnie and you are quite likely to end up in the refrigeration room.

Talking about talking and crying, did you see that I have made Joe Nhlanhla Deputy Minister with Responsibility for the Co-ordination of Intelligence? Frankly it was General Meiring who persuaded me to make the appointment. He said Intelligence was too important to be left in the control of soldiers, which I thought was very humble of him. He said Joe was uniquely qualified because of his experience as head of ANC security during the years of exile. The only trouble with Joe is that I have never actually heard him talk. I have tried talking to him on several occasions, but all that happens is that tears well up in his eyes and he starts frantically sucking his thumb. Meiring says it is the mark of a master-spy; that he is privy to so many secrets he does not dare speak in case he inadvertently lets one out. Jomo says he was in fact struck dumb by fright when he was first appointed head of ANC security. I am never sure when Jomo is joking.

A lot of my time has been taken up with entertaining a British minister called Michael Heseltine. He is another strange man. For some reason he introduces himself to everyone as Lord Greystoke. When he heard that President Mitterrand had been to Khayelitsha he insisted on going as well. He arrived carrying a huge bag over his shoulder. It was full of coloured beads which he insisted on handing out to everyone with a pat to the head. He kept asking where the jungle had gone. He told one old lady that he would be sending an expert out from London to teach everyone how to make fire, so they could learn how to cook.

The managing director of one of these telephone companies was with us and he presented him with a drum which he said was an African cellular phone. Heseltine looked very knowledgeable at this. The last I saw of him he was heading off in the British ambassador's Rolls Royce, banging away happily in the back seat, stopping every now and then to stick his head out of the window. And this all happened in the morning; heaven knows what he gets up to in the noonday sun.

I have been very unfair to Thabo. You will remember I said he had gone missing? Well it turns out he is engaged in the struggle. I do not know if I told you about this, but the King of Morocco promised some time ago that he would pay the ANC's election expenses. Ever since our great victory Thabo has been sending him invoices. Apparently the King keeps telling everyone that he had his fingers crossed when he made the promise. Anyway Thabo, after endless unsuccessful attempts to get an audience with His Majesty, flew to Rabat, marched into the palace and, announcing he had come to see the King, sat himself down in the royal antechamber. He has been there a week now. Mike Louw says the National Intelligence Service is busy building him a portable lavatory disguised to look like a government dispatch box. No greater love has man than this; that he should lay down his life to squeeze a few rand out of the King of Morocco.

Your tearless comrade,
Nelson

Mrs Mandela was widely believed to have participated in the murder of a young anti-apartheid activist, "Stompie" Moeketsi — suspected by her of being a police informer. She was given a suspended sentence by the supreme court for conspiracy to kidnap the boy after the judge reluctantly accepted an alibi she offered. In August she delivered an extraordinary "maiden" speech to Parliament in which she reiterated her innocence of any wrongdoing and denounced the court's finding. She also made remarks about the selfless sacrifices of womenfolk in the liberation cause which struck a particular chord, because of press disclosures as to her own adultery during her husband's years of imprisonment.

Tokyo Sexwale, ANC Premier of Gauteng province incorporating South Africa's industrial heartland, including Johannesburg and Pretoria, nurses presidential aspirations which show little chance of being realised. He has been the target of rumours about links with the Nigerian "mafia" which are presumed to be untrue. He has claimed the said mafia are intent on destroying him, because of his hostility towards the drugs trade.

OFFICE OF THE PRESIDENT

August 19 1994

Dear Walter,

My apologies for taking so long to write, but I have been very busy thanks in large part to Winnie. We tried to persuade her that her maiden speech had to be non-controversial — to talk about the sardine industry, or something like that. But, no, it had to be about Winnie. You have probably read about it in the press: weeping and wailing over the fate of Stompie and her helplessness to save him; denunciations of the "apartheid court" for "criminalising" her and leering references to other MPs whose "hands are dripping with blood". The reaction was predictable: pandemonium, with that little man from Houghton leaping on his desk and waving feverishly to Frene Ginwala in the Speaker's chair, demanding Winnie be thrown out for using parliamentary privilege to smear the courts. It was all very embarrassing to me, personally. Corbett sat in judgment on Winnie and I've just made him Chief Justice for another three years. And now here is my wife denouncing him as a murdering apartheid judge.

Frene told the House that she would have to think about it for a while and disappeared into a back room, emerging half an hour later to announce triumphantly there was no problem, because Winnie had been smearing the apartheid courts and, as apartheid was dead, so were the courts and therefore they could not be smeared. This was met by cheers and tears of jubilation from Winnie's supporters, but you can imagine how it must have gone down in Bloemfontein; I mean these judges do seem catatonic at times, but no-one likes to be pronounced dead before his time, even if it is by the Speaker.

The next day Winnie came running excitedly into my office, dragging two men behind her and shouting that Frene was right, that she had scientific proof for it. She then introduced me to one of the men with her, a Professor Something-or-other who, it turned out, is her chief adviser as Deputy Minister of Science. He shuffled uneasily from foot to foot, wiped his pebble-glasses and then mumbled that it was true, we were all different people. After more mumbling it emerged he was saying all the cells in every person's body are replaced by new cells over a 10-year period so that, in effect, we become a totally different person once a decade. Winnie then introduced me to the other man, who had a squashed face that looked as if he had run into the back of too many ambulances in his time. He turned out to be her lawyer and he solemnly declared that the scientific facts had to be recognised by the law. He said he had already issued a string of libel writs on Winnie's behalf, because she was not the same Winnie as had (or had not) helped beat Stompie to death. I objected that it happened less than 10 years ago and Winnie cut in to point out that it was more than five years ago and we all believed in majority rule, didn't we? Well, I'm a democrat, Walter, but I must say the implications of this are rather disturbing. Although it does help explain FW de Klerk ...

Anyway Winnie hurried off, saying she had an urgent meeting with the country's top scientists to discuss hormone therapy which could speed up the rate of cell replacement. Apparently she's hoping that she will then be able to sue the newspapers that recently accused her of filching funds from the ANC Welfare Department, as well as some magazine which has just voted her "Rear-End-of-a-Donkey-of-the-Month" (or something like that).

One crisis fades and another looms. Heaven knows what is happening in the PWV. Out of the blue Tokyo Sexwale's office announces he is the target of a diabolical plot to destroy him devised by gonorrhoea-infected, Mafia-linked, neo-Nazi drug barons. It is very much off the record, but I have been advised the plot has already gone into operation. Basie Smit says the drug barons have kidnapped Tokyo's Aunt Edith's dachshund called "Wors" and have sent an ear to her in the post with a note written in blood saying she'll get the other one if her nephew fails to build a mandrax refinery under the Reconstruction and Development Programme. Jessie Duarte has taken all the region's police off uniform duty and has them disguised as SPCA inspectors combing the country for a one-eared dachshund which may have a drug problem. The question I keep asking everyone is: why are they picking on poor Tokyo?

My first 100 days in office are up this week. It feels like 100 years.

Love to all at home,

Nelson

S outh Africa's major newspaper group, the Argus — under its new proprietor, the Irish rugby player and tomato sauce magnate, Tony O'Reilly — ran a series of exclusive but confusing stories relating to a mysterious substance called "red mercury". The chemical make-up of the substance was never conclusively identified, but it was said to have been isolated by Russian scientists in the closing days of the Soviet empire and used in the manufacture of miniature nuclear bombs.

A large contingent of soldiers from Umkhonto weSizwe (MK), the ANC's guerrilla army, marched on the Union Buildings to protest against their treatment under a programme intended to integrate them with the new South African National Defence Force (SANDF). The demonstrators dispersed after speaking to Mandela and his Deputy Minister of Defence, Ronnie Kasrils.

OFFICE OF THE PRESIDENT

September 16 1994

Dear Walter,

There were scenes of great excitement here at the weekend. Jomo came running into my bedroom on Friday night just as I was settling into bed with a copy of *War and Peace*, shouting: "The Russians are coming; the Russians are coming ..."

I could not understand his agitation, because the Russians came here a long time ago. You cannot move nowadays without falling over them flogging the last secrets of the Soviet Empire, truckloads of red mercury, or pen-sized nuclear bombs with free subscriptions to *The Star*.

But Jomo knows the Russians. At least, he occasionally makes noises like a lovelorn moose sighing for a lost mate which he claims is fluent Russian. And it was in a state of high agitation that he locked me into the Libertas toilet which is designed to take a direct hit from three nuclear bombs without flushing.

Fortunately the little window at the back was unlocked and I clambered out. There was chaos outside, officials and soldiers running in all directions shouting for Joe Modise. They seemed to have forgotten Joe was overseas. He is meant to be buying ships from the British. But from the little he seems to have learned about naval matters — he keeps mixing up gunboats with aircraft carriers, which is playing havoc with our Defence budget — I suspect he is spending his time lurking around Bond Street, indulging his peculiar passion for crocodile-skin jungle-boots.

A bit embarrassed in my dressing gown and slippers — and a red bonnet left behind by Marike de Klerk which Jomo had for some reason thrust on my head — I wandered over to the Union Buildings to see what was happening.

They were not Russians after all. They were MK soldiers — about 500 of them, milling around on the lawns of Union Buildings. They seemed a bit taken aback when they saw me appear in Marike's bonnet, but when they recognised me underneath it they all started toyi-toyiing and shouting "Mandela for President, Down with Apartheid". This went on for a while until someone remembered that I was President and silence fell. It was a tense moment; you know how unnerving it can be when people run out of conversation. The troops were shuffling from feet to feet and fingering the triggers on their bazookas while I fiddled with Marike's bonnet which kept falling over one eye. Then I suddenly felt a slap on my shoulder.

I am 76 years old, Walter, so when I say I had one of the biggest frights of my life you will appreciate the awful vision which confronted me. Ronnie Kasrils can be disturbing enough a sight as it is, with those writhing eyebrows which someone once described as Mopani worms engaged in carnal combat. To make matters worse, in an attempt to impress the generals he has had the little hair left to him shorn down into what is presumably intended to be a crew cut, but looks more like the remains of Delville Wood after the Germans had finished with it.

When I turned around I was confronted with this figure dressed in black, with what looked like the inner tube of a bicycle tyre wrapped around his head, standing frozen in the position of some ghastly "living statue" — one foot raised in front of him, clutching what appeared to be two metal stars above his head. Our Deputy Minister of Defence has become a Ninja man, Walter!

Well I must say, despite the palpitations his appearance caused me, it is useful having a Ninja man in the Defence Ministry. In no time at all he had pulled out a small delegation from the troops and had the rest enthusiastically doing press-ups on the lawn. He then led the way to my office, where all ended peacefully. I dug out a couple of bottles of KWV brandy which De Klerk had left hidden behind a filing cabinet and the soldiers poured out their grievances. I will not go into them here, Walter — the usual litany about itchy bed socks, a shortage of shiny medals and frustration at being forced to sit through *The Longest Day* every Saturday night in the camp cinema. I promised the Cabinet would give the issues serious consideration and, after Ronnie had lent them the bus fare, they headed off home.

I was left wondering whether it would not be worth turning the whole SANDF into Ninja men. I am sure Robert Mugabe would be pleased.

Best wishes,
Nelson

*T*he early months of the Mandela administration were marked by controversy over the incomes of politicians — critics charging that MPs were on a "gravy train" and MPs protesting that they did not earn enough to discharge their responsibilities. Archbishop Desmond Tutu was particularly critical of the gravy train.

The continuing power struggle between the leaders of the Zulus was marked by the efforts of Chief Buthelezi to force the capitulation of his nephew, King Goodwill Zwelithini, by starving him of funds. The use of bulls' testicles as a currency of exchange may come as a surprise to ethnographers, being previously unrecorded.

The Reed Dance is an ancient festival, the precursor to the debutante's ball at which young maidens "come out" socially in England.

OFFICE OF THE PRESIDENT

September 23 1994

Dear Walter,

The art of government, I am beginning to learn, is not dealing with the masses, but with the so-called leaders. I mean your average shanty dweller in Khayelitsha just goes about his or her business without any fuss, fighting for their dinner with the local rabid dogs, bathing, brushing their teeth and doing the laundry in the occasional puddle. They cause me no problems, make no demands on my time.

But I just have to step out of Tuynhuys and I disappear under a pile of MPs and Cabinet ministers, clawing at my suit with torn and filthy fingernails, rattling tins in my face, croaking appeals for food for their starving children and a year's free parking at DF Malan airport.

And those are just the politicians. As for kings, they are a full-time occupation. From which you will no doubt gather that I have been having trouble with Zwelithini again.

It all started at a cocktail party a few weeks ago when the King came sidling up to me and whispered that he could let me have a couple of seats at the Shaka Day festivities at a special discount.

These are difficult times for royalty, so it was in a charitable frame of mind that I slipped a few rand to the King in exchange for a couple of bulls' testicles which apparently pass for theatre tickets in his part of the world.

I had quite forgotten the incident when out of the blue, last week, Gatsha came storming into Cabinet and began shouting that I had insulted the shades of his ancestral spirits and threatened the very existence of the Zulu nation by buying tickets for Shaka Day from the King. Which was all very confusing until my Education Minister, Bengu — who, as you know, is a Zulu as well — hissed in my ear that Gatsha traditionally took a 20% rake-off on Shaka Day tickets. A bit reluctantly (it is embarrassing to load one's pockets down with bulls' testicles) I took Gatsha to one side during the Cabinet tea break and slipped him a few rand for a couple more tickets. He went off, mumbling something about unnatural relations between Xhosas and the canine population, and for the umpteenth time I made a mental vow to stay out of Zulu affairs.

But it was not to be. A couple of days later I was settling down in my study, hoping for a few minutes of quiet in which to finish page two of *War and Peace,* when the phone began jangling. I picked it up and heard Zwelithini on the other end shouting for help before the line was cut off. There was nothing for it but to take a helicopter down to Nongoma to see what was going on.

It was an extraordinary sight that met us when we landed at the King's kraal: the royal mud hut surrounded by thousands of nude Zulu girls, all waving reeds over their heads.

It turned out it was the time of the annual Reed Dance when Zulu virgins descend on the royal kraal to pay homage to their lord and master. Ethnologists claim, curiously, that the girls carry these reeds as an avowal of maidenly innocence. It is said there is a tradition that if a girl's reed bends in the wind it means she has been dallying injudiciously beside some footpath.

But if you examine these wands they are, quite frankly, rigid and the symbolism as these girls waved them suggestively in the direction of the King's hut seemed quite clear to me.

Certainly my view was shared by the King, whom I found gibbering with terror in the corner of his hut, surrounded by 15 exasperated wives. When he saw me Zwelithini threw himself into my arms and sobbed out his sorry tale.

It transpired that, in a desperate effort to prop up a dwindling royal treasury, he had been overbooking for Shaka Day. As a result he had been forced to skip the morning ration of bulls' testicles which he had been devouring with his porridge since childhood to ensure he became an upstanding figure of a king. This deficiency in his diet, coupled with advancing middle age, had so undermined his confidence that, when he saw the maidenly hordes advancing on the kraal in pursuit of their annual tribute, his nerve had suddenly broken.

At 76 I was really in no position to help him. And when he looked up and saw that helplessness in my eyes he gave a final shriek and leapt out of the door. The last sight I had of the Zulu sovereign was of him disappearing over a distant kopje, pursued by baying regiments of naked virgins symbolically waving broken reeds over their heads.

It was a relief to get back to Cape Town, to find the quiet and calm figure of a British Prime Minister waiting for me.

I know you are anxious to hear all about Major, but frankly there is not much to tell. He is a very characterless individual. So much so that it is difficult at times to distinguish between his face and the back of his head. After a while one gets used to speaking to the side wearing the spectacles.

In his speech to Parliament — delivered with much windmilling of his arms and huffing and puffing — he made a great thing about winds of change blowing in Africa. Listening to him my mind went back to the terrible suffering of the Zulu King in the name of tradition and I thought to myself: "Not really."

Best wishes,
Nelson

*I*n September 1994 South African television viewers were startled by a physical confrontation in the Johannesburg studios of the SABC between Chief Buthelezi and a spokesman for King Goodwill Zwelithini, Prince Sifiso Zulu. The chief, who said he had wandered into the studio during a live broadcast by mistake, claimed the prince had drawn a concealed gun in an attempt to assassinate him.

The Shell House massacre saw eight supporters of Buthelezi's Inkatha Freedom Party shot dead while demonstrating outside the ANC's Johannesburg headquarters shortly before the 1994 majority rule elections.

OFFICE OF THE PRESIDENT

September 30 1994

Dear Walter,

Do you ever find your dreams getting mixed up with reality? It has started happening to me with nightmares. On Sunday I fell asleep in my armchair reading page three of *War and Peace* when I started dreaming of Gatsha.

I was sitting in an SABC television studio, assuring Freek Robinson that I thought King Zwelithini was one of the greatest monarchs that had ever lived and that I secretly dreamed all my life of being a Zulu warrior, when the door burst open and Gatsha came leaping in, monkey skins flying, brandishing an assegai and yelling: "He's my King, he's my King." He then proceeded to chase me round and round the studio, jabbing at me with his assegai while Freek wailed: "Gentlemen, please, we can return to this later, but now we have to take a commercial break."

Then the police came rushing into the studio and Gatsha pointed at me, shouting: "He tried to assassinate me, he tried to assassinate me." I said: "But Gatsha, you know I would never hurt you." He screamed back: "He lies, I've never met him in my life before, I came in here to have a cup of tea with my royal uncle twice removed who is

directly descended from Cetshwayo when this man tried to assassinate me with a water pistol loaded with dum-dum bullets." The police
then demanded to see my passbook. When I failed to produce it, they
put handcuffs on me and dragged me out of the door while Freek was
putting a microphone on Gatsha and asking him what he thought of
the Shell House massacre.

At that moment I was woken up by the crash of *War and Peace*
falling on to the floor. A bit shaken I switched on the television only
to see Gatsha in a television studio jumping up and down on some
bewildered man, shouting: "He tried to assassinate me, he tried to
assassinate me, this fraudulent prince that hasn't a drop of
Cetshwayo's blood in his veins and who I have never met in my life
before has a loaded starting pistol in his pocket and my bodyguard
never put it in there."

Convinced that I was still dreaming I staggered out of the study,
falling over Jomo who was sleeping on the floor outside the door as
usual. It turned out he was having a nightmare about Gatsha chas-
ing him around his dacha on the Black Sea with an assegai and he
leapt to his feet and rushed out of the front door screaming in
Russian: "The Zulus are coming, the Zulus are coming, run for the
gravy train ..." This started the domestic staff chanting: "The gravy
train, the gravy train's coming" and the whole pack of them went
toyi-toyiing down the driveway into the night after Jomo, flattening
Archbishop Desmond Tutu who was just walking in the gate. I
helped the archbishop to his feet and dusted him down murmuring
apologies. But he just said scornfully: "The gravy train again!" and
stalked off after them.

I was settling down to *War and Peace* again when there was a
banging on the front door. I opened it to find a squad of policeman
armed with assault rifles and bazookas outside. I started protesting
that I had not had time to find my passbook when one of them thrust a
piece of paper at me. It was a writ issued by Gatsha demanding
immediate payment of R80-million for gunning down his supporters
at Shell House in an attempt to rob him of votes in the general election and deprive him of his ancestral right to be President as well as
Prime Minister.

I don't know why Gatsha keeps doing these things to me. I have always been very nice to him and have urged others to do the same, explaining that the unfortunate circumstances of his childhood made him the way he is and he can hardly be blamed for that. Whenever I see him I make a point of hugging and embracing him, even though it is a nuisance having to have all my pockets sewn up.

Pleasant dreams, old friend,
Nelson

P*resident Mandela's visit to the United States coincided with reports of a power struggle between the South African ambassador to Washington and the South African ambassador to the United Nations in New York, both of whom apparently regarded themselves as the senior diplomat.*

OFFICE OF THE PRESIDENT

October 14 1994

Dear Walter,

They call the United States the powerhouse of the world, but it struck me as more of a madhouse. And it seems to be infectious.

The signs were there, from the moment my plane touched down at New York, but I failed to recognise them. I was clambering down the stairs when suddenly two men came rolling down the red carpet towards me. At first I thought it was some sort of acrobatic act, put on for my benefit — you know how the Americans are big on show business? So I stopped and started politely clapping when I realised I was the only one doing so.

I looked a bit more closely and saw they were none other than our ambassador to Washington, Harold Schwarz, and our ambassador to the United Nations, James Steward, apparently trying to chew each other's leg off. Jomo, who was just behind me, assumed it was an outbreak of rabies and began unzipping the guitar case he was carrying, to put them out of their misery with his AK-47.

Before he could do so the two ambassadors, who by now had rolled up to my feet, seemed to realise I was there. They leapt up, chorused "Welcome Mr President" and to my astonishment both grabbed at my hand and began playing some variation on "one potato, two potato ... " — you know, that game the grandchildren like so much? After a few minutes of this they seemed to tire of it and started shouting at each other " ... I was first ... No, I was ... Washington's the capital, so yeahhh ... New York's bigger, so yah, boo, sucks ... " This exchange seemed to excite them to action once more and, bellowing oaths, they fell upon each other again, mercifully rolling out of sight behind the waiting VIPs.

Naturally I tried to pass it off in front of my hosts as nothing more than the hurly-burly of public life, but it all left me a bit shaken. I was whisked off to the home of a very powerful businessman, a Mr Rockefeller, and after greeting him I went off to have a bit of a lie-down in order to sooth my nerves. But I had no sooner put my head on the pillow than the telephone began jangling on the bedside table.

I picked it up and a coy voice said: "This is Peter Pan here." I explained that he seemed to have the wrong number and replaced the phone. But my head had no sooner touched the pillow again than it started its jangling once more. The same voice on the other end said: "Is Tinker Bell there?" Considerably confused I said no, I knew of no Mrs Bell. At this the voice began crying: "Clap your hands, clap your hands, or the fairies will die."

I hurriedly put the telephone down again and was trying to figure out how to get myself a much-needed sherry when it started up again. I was tempted not to answer it, but fearful that it might be a matter of national interest back home, picked it up. It turned out to be Elizabeth Taylor pleading with me between hiccups to be nice to her friend Michael Jackson who was just a lost little boy and not to believe the foul libels being put around by Captain Hook.

The upshot was that I had to spend an hour on the telephone listening to some pop star babbling on about his plans to build Never-Never Land in an abandoned fortress he had found on a hill outside Pretoria.

After making a hurried call to Winnie, to tell her to keep the grandchildren away from the Voortrekker Monument in future, I had to rush out to a banquet. There a man called Marion Barry, who claimed to be the rightful mayor of Washington, kept nudging me in the ribs and whispering: "We ex-convicts must stick together, eh!" while pushing packets of what appeared to be castor sugar into my pocket. Then there was an ex-presidential candidate, Jesse Jackson, who insisted on throwing his arms around my neck every time he saw a photographer lift his camera. By the time I staggered back to Rockefeller's home, my pockets stuffed full of sugar and my neck feeling as if I had been scrumming against Uli Schmidt, I was longing to be taken away by the men in white coats.

What a relief it was to arrive back at Waterkloof yesterday to be met by a mournful-looking Joe Modise with the news that there was a rebellion in the armed forces and the entire public service was about to go on strike. Home at last, home at last; thank God Almighty I'm home at last!

Yours as ever,
Nelson

A llan Boesak, the leader of the ANC in the Western Cape, was appointed South Africa's ambassador to the United Nations in Geneva, but fell victim to scandal over the alleged misuse of foreign aid funds. Some of the money was alleged to have been diverted to his wife's film company.

**THE PALACE,
RIYADH,
SAUDI ARABIA**

November 4 1994

Dear Walter,

Thank heaven the Nats did not discover this place before the April elections.

I was met at the airport, as was to be expected, by some sort of prince. I assumed he was a prince although I must say that under the tent he was wearing he might as well have been a circus midget on horseback. He made a strange clanking noise as he advanced upon me down the priceless red silk carpet. At first I thought he might be some sort of mechanical man, but it subsequently transpired that it was the gold ingots with which princes in these parts bedeck them-selves. There are some very rich people here, Walter.

A motorcade was waiting for me outside the airport. And what a motorcade! One thing you must admire about the Saudis: for all their riches they have not lost touch with their roots. Behind our vehicle were four convertible stretch-limousines in which rode three camels and a donkey.

After the prince had been lifted into our limousine with a crane (their jewellery must be very heavy) I tried to make conversation with him. I had to shout, because it was a very stretched limousine.

I had been warned by Foreign Affairs to be very careful about what questions one asks these people. The Saudis are notoriously sensitive and carry grudges for a long time, which can play havoc with the price of petrol. So I bellowed as politely as I could an inquiry as to how many people lived in their glorious country.

I could sense immediately that I was going to have to ask Pik Botha to start refilling our mine-shafts with oil and reduce the national speed limit again. It seems that the most provocative question one can ask a Saudi is the number of people living in the kingdom. The reason is that they have brought so many foreigners into the country — Filipinos, Palestinians, Eskimos, Yaks and heaven knows who else — to work as their servants that the Saudis themselves have become hopelessly outnumbered.

Terrified that someone will make trouble for them by mentioning majority rule they have tried to keep this unfortunate fact secret by outlawing censuses. Anyone seen counting people is immediately decapitated. In fact it is advisable in Saudi Arabia to pretend you can't count at all. Ask a passerby the time around here and they assume you are the secret police. They start confessing to the most extraordinary things while anxiously clutching their heads. It can be very disconcerting.

I finally arrived at the prince's palace to find a pile of frantic faxes, telexes and telegrams. Half the messages seemed to be complaints from South African actors that they had not been given parts in the remake of *Ben-Hur* that Allan Boesak is apparently working on with sponsorship from the Swedish International Development Agency. The rest were complaints from the Swedes, because Boesak had promised to use the money to make a film with Bergman on how to dig a borehole with one spade and a plumb-line.

In the evening I struck up an unexpected friendship with the prince who, it turns out, is a sad figure. To listen to him is to realise that money is not everything. For one thing, as a devout Saudi he cannot drink alcohol. For another he has a genetic predisposition to excess perspiration which is why, as he explained, he drinks large quantities of eau de cologne.

At first he mixed the stuff with tonic and a touch of bitters, but after several glasses he began downing it neat by the bottle. He then began weeping and told me a piteous story of how he landed up with his harem.

It seems that from his childhood, due to some confusion over a eunuch, he thought beautiful women always had beards — a notion of which time failed to disabuse him, because in Saudi Arabia one only discovers whether one's loved one sports a beard when you marry her. He said his love life had been reduced to one of those street games involving three thimbles and a bean in which one is endlessly lifting the wrong thimble in frustrated search for the bean.

He had got up to the hideous discovery he made on defrocking his 3 241st wife when I was unable to take the fumes any more. Making my excuses I retired to bed where, before succumbing to sweet dreams of heavenly, beardless *houris* dancing around date palms in a remote *wadi,* I pondered just how lucky we are in South Africa where people count.

Wish you were here,
Nelson

A *fter complaints from the ANC that national television was giving insufficient coverage to the presidency, the SABC promised
to pay special attention to Mandela's activities.*

*At about this time, a fuss developed between the Johannesburg Press
Club and the Minister of Water Affairs, Kader Asmal. The minister
returned a gold medal which he had collected on behalf of Mandela as
"News Maker of the Year", saying the club had insulted the President
by complaining at his failure to turn up personally. Mysteriously, the
Press Club said they had not presented anyone with a gold medal and
had planned to give the President a carving in indigenous wood. They
said the gold medal appeared to have been presented by the Gold Reef
City entertainment complex.*

OFFICE OF THE PRESIDENT

November 8 1994

Dear Walter,

The suffering of the Princess of Wales at the hands of the paparazzi is
nothing compared with what I am going through with SABC. Some
idiot at Auckland Park decided it was necessary to film and broadcast
all my public appearances.

There is now an outside broadcast unit permanently stationed at
the front gate. Every time the wind blows there are screams and bangs
as cameramen come tumbling out of the surrounding jacaranda trees.
My bodyguards have opened fire several times on directional micro-
phones being poked over the perimeter wall, which they mistake for
snipers' rifles.

I just have to stick my head out the window and on go the flood-
lights as the cameras start grinding, Lester Venter leaping up and
down behind them like an outsize bag of jelly-beans shrieking to his
audience: "There he is folks, there he is !!!" It is enough to give anyone bulimia.

I have to be stoical about it, because relations with the press have deteriorated somewhat recently, largely as a result of that little Indian lawyer, Kader Asmal. You may remember that I made him Minister of the Waterworks, or something like that. I suspect he may have been disappointed at the appointment; he likes to be in the limelight and the state of the country's waterworks does not seem to interest the press greatly.

So what he did was set up a special task force, made up largely of out-of-work journalists, and gave them the job of renaming all the country's dams. He disappeared with them for several months. Apparently in the highest traditions of investigative journalism, the task force insisted on touring the country in a fleet of government Mercedes, staying at five-star hotels and only venturing out of the bar to descend in a giggling mob on the nearest dam wall in order to bash it with empty champagne bottles shouting: "God bless all who sail in her."

Eventually they ran out of whiskey supplies, or dams to name, and I began to notice Kader hanging around at the back of the crowd at press conferences, gazing wistfully at the television cameras. Feeling a little sorry for him I asked him one day, a few weeks ago, to stand in for me at one of these tiresome Press Club luncheons where I was to be named News Maker of the Year for the 1 000th time.

Unfortunately Kader in his excitement got the function rooms mixed up and went to a lunch organised by Gold Reef City instead. He was allowed in, apparently being mistaken for a waiter. He then proceeded to guzzle someone else's lunch at the high table before marching to the podium and embarking on a lengthy speech about the revolutionary achievement of the ANC in renaming all the country's dams.

He got only to half-way through the speech when the organisers, convinced they had a mad waiter on their hands, moved to seize the microphone. After a short struggle the Gold Reef chairman, Solly Krog, gained possession of the instrument and attempted light-heartedly to smooth over the incident with a remark about "strangers masquerading as Nelson Mandela". This incensed Kader, who took it for a slighting reference to my failure to turn up.

Shouting "you have insulted the President of the Republic", he grabbed a newly struck Gold Reef City gold coin which was lying in state on the high table — under the misapprehension it was intended as a presentation for me — and stormed out the door, to be pursued down Commissioner Street by besuited businessmen crying "Stop thief!"

Somehow he eluded them and returned to his office, immediately issuing a press statement on Ministry of Waterworks-headed note-paper denouncing the Press Club and announcing that he was return-ing their gold medal as a protest on my behalf at their shocking behaviour.

This caused some confusion among members of the Press Club, whose function had passed off amidst scenes of much drunkenness in the course of which they had presented a whiskey bottle carved out of yellow-wood and stinkwood to a bewildered Indian waiter under the misapprehension that he was the Minister of Waterworks. I am having to consider the appointment of a commission of inquiry to sort the whole mess out.

Yours as ever,
Nelson

The police, still living in apparent ignorance of the transition to majority rule, continued to treat the ANC as a terrorist organisation, routinely arresting or shooting up its leaders. Mandela had a crisis meeting with the country's 11 most senior officers to try and explain to them the realpolitik of post-liberation South Africa. He reported afterwards that he was well received and was satisfied he had the "full support" of the force's commanders — a claim received with some scepticism.

Deputy President Thabo Mbeki also hit out at the police, claiming the crime wave in the country was a figment of their collective imagination.

The 1994 Miss World competition was staged in South Africa — at Sun City, a casino centre and theme park owned and devised by Sol Kerzner.

General Johan van der Merwe was South Africa's Police Commissioner.

A group of African-Americans in Harlem announced plans to crown Winnie Mandela Queen of Africa. There was some speculation that it was a practical joke, but she graciously announced she was accepting the post.

OFFICE OF THE PRESIDENT

November 15 1994

Dear Walter,

I know I have written to you about this before, but I am becoming increasingly concerned about the rise of monarchism in our republic. Yes, I know, Gatsha has struck a blow for the people by proclaiming King Goodwill a chief. But he was always one to stand against the tide of human history.

As you may have seen, down in the Eastern Cape Raymond Mhlaba has announced that all paramount chiefs will henceforth be known as kings. I walked into Winnie's office a couple of days ago to find her on her knees on the floor, surrounded by photographs of the British crown jewels. She is apparently determined that her coronation as Queen of Africa in Harlem next year will outsparkle anything the world has seen before.

Our Sun King, Sol Kerzner, is flogging South Africa abroad as the "Kingdom in the Sun"; I met 87 beauty queens he has inveigled out here from various parts of the world with hints of marriage to local monarchs. I did not mind having to kiss them all, but three delivered rather painful blows to my shoulder with their wooden sceptres in an apparent attempt to knight me. I just hope the bruises will have gone by the time Queen Elizabeth comes trotting down the gangplank and starts banging away on my shoulder with Excalibur.

All the royal goings-on have at least provided a break from the trouble I have been having with the police. It is not so much that the police have declared war on the ANC; it is more of a turkey-shoot. It is almost impossible to get an ANC official into a vehicle nowadays, they are so terrified of being shot for speeding, or having electrodes tied to their extremities in an effort to make them confess to drunken and disorderly driving.

Thabo has been trying to hit back, by accusing the generals of being alarmists about crime. He went so far as to tell a conference of foreign investors this week that there was no crime at all in South Africa; they were just scare stories made up by the generals in an effort to get funding for their pensions. Unfortunately three of the foreign investors had been raped on the way to the conference, 15 had been mugged and seven failed to turn up at all, having been unavoidably detained at the Cape Town mortuary.

I did try to smooth things over with the generals by inviting them to talks. I got a message back, scrawled in somebody's blood, agreeing to meet me at the Johan Van der Merwe Third Force Memorial Centre outside Pretoria on condition that Jomo left his bazooka at home.

When I got there I was heavily frisked and my two hearing-aids confiscated under the misapprehension that they were tape recorders secreted on my person by Judge Goldstone in an effort to implicate them in Yugoslavian war crimes.

Unfortunately this meant the meeting had to be conducted by sign language. But I made a most conciliatory speech, inviting them to take their rightful places under black command in the new South Africa. This was greeted with scenes of what I took to be great enthusiasm — bemedalled generals jumping on the tables, waving chairs in the air and firing shots into the ceiling with their service revolvers.

I then went to meet the press in the canteen. After Parks — you remember Parks, my press spokesman? — had dragged them out from under the tables and behind the fridge, where several had taken refuge, I was able to tell them that I had received a standing ovation from the police command and that all was well in our beautiful land.

Sorry to have to finish writing this on toilet paper, but they have refused to allow me any writing materials, as well as taking away my shoe-laces and braces.

I can hear Mike, my driver, down the corridor still denying between screams that he crossed an unbroken white line as he pulled away from the Johan Van der Merwe Third Force Memorial Centre. But I suspect they will get a confession out of him in the end.

You know, Walter, I am quite looking forward to seeing the old lime quarry again. At least I will not be troubled by royalty there.

With best wishes,

Nelson

OFFICE OF THE PRESIDENT

December 9 1994

Dear Walter,

I have been distracted over the past week by the imminent publication of my autobiography. I had quite forgotten that I was writing it and no doubt you have been unaware of it as well.

You will remember how I used to keep a diary on the Island, recording the number of press-ups I had done each day and other routine observations with which one whiles away time in prison — as to the frequency of one's bowel movements and the number of lumps one has discovered in the morning's porridge? Well, when I was released from Victor Verster, word somehow spread about the existence of the diary, causing great excitement in the publishing world.

My old friend Fatima Meer decided that we should sell it and an auction was arranged in London. After some fierce bidding it eventually went to an American company labouring under the name of Little Brown, for the sum of $1,8-million. I duly handed the precious document to them, but it transpired that it was insufficient for their needs. In fact, they became quite aggressive about the number of dollars they had had to pay for each lump in my porridge, not to mention other sightings.

After some terse transatlantic exchanges, a deal was thrashed out by which they hired a New York journalist for some $300 000 to write my autobiography on my behalf. It seemed a rather strange arrangement to me, but it appears it is a firm tradition in the US for people to write other people's autobiographies, those important enough to write their own customarily being illiterate.

The choice of the author also seemed strange: a young man whose name constantly escapes me, but who is apparently the world authority on takkies, which are known in the US as sneakers. I was assured, however, that these items of foot apparel are central to American culture and that he was ideally qualified for the job.

Lumps in the porridge seemingly being insufficient to inspire this young man's creative drive, he took to following me around clutching a tape recorder. He appeared to share Joe Modise's affection for footwear and obviously used his $300 000 to indulge his perverse passion by donning a new pair of takkies each day, which squeaked horribly as he pursued me. Irritated beyond measure by the noise, I tended to answer him a little brusquely and at times no doubt thoughtlessly. The result is this appalling autobiography, which I suspect will haunt me for the rest of my days.

It is not that the book is untrue; it is more that it is a gloss on my life. "Airbrushed" is, I believe, the word used in the US.

Take the account it gives of my circumcision. In bare outline it is reasonable enough: a group of my youthful contemporaries and I were made to sit naked in a clearing — watched by parents, aunts, uncles, chiefs, kings and anyone else who could afford the entrance fee — while we awaited the ministrations of the *ingcibi*, the circumcision expert.

But the book then has this elderly man skilfully performing the operation with an assegai, each one of us responding bravely to the painful cut with a cry of "*Ndiyindoda* [I am a man]". Now this is all very romantic, but quite untrue.

The *ingcibi* was elderly, but he wielded an axe. We all had to stare straight in front, but I remember the initial thud of the instrument followed by the cries of the first boy: "Help! Police!! Fire brigade!!!!" This was followed by a succession of further thumps and then the rasping of a stone on metal as the axeman belatedly sharpened the blade.

The second boy cried out not "*Ndiyindoda*", but "Aaaaiinnaaaahh". A silence fell on the clearing, broken by the old man mumbling: "It was too long, anyway." I blacked out for a couple of minutes, so I do not know what happened to the next two, although I did hear that in later years they were in demand among male voice choirs for soprano parts.

You know, Walter, I have often been asked over the years how I discovered the courage and the stoicism to face a possible death sentence so impassively at Rivonia and endure all those years of incarceration without a whimper. The answer is a simple one: after circumcision life has seemed very easy.

I came around from my momentary blackout to find myself staring straight into the squint and frantic eyes of the *ingcibi*. With one hand he was heaving on my foreskin. From the difficulty he was having with the other, in raising the blood-spattered axe above his head, he was clearly suffering from an advanced case of Parkinson's disease.

The axe fell. I looked down. The ancestral spirits were with me and my dearly departed part wasn't.

"I remember walking differently on that day, straighter, taller, firmer," records my autobiography. I thought I was doubled over for a week. But then who am I to quarrel with my memoirs ?

Yours fondly,
Nelson

T*he Zimbabwean President, Robert Mugabe, whose erratic administration has largely wrecked his country's economy, was reported to have travelled to South Africa in December for medical treatment. But on his return to Harare he told reporters he had just been in Cape Town on a holiday.*

At the ANC's biennial conference, meanwhile, it was reported that the party was unable to account for large sums of money donated to it by sympathisers.

It also emerged on the eve of the conference that Winnie Mandela had been involved in a mysterious diamond deal in Angola. The Angolan President, Eduardo dos Santos, denied allegations that he was involved. Mrs Mandela had previously been linked to the diamond trade through her friendship with a convicted IDB (illicit diamond-buying) crook, Hazel Crane, who gave the President's wife a house in Cape Town and claimed to have been paying for her clothes and groceries.

OFFICE OF THE PRESIDENT

December 19 1994

Dear Walter,

It was wonderful seeing you in Bloemfontein, even if it was only briefly. There was in fact something of a panic on; for a moment I thought we were going to have to call the whole conference off and declare a national state of emergency.

It all started when we received word from Harare that President Mugabe had fallen victim to the bubonic plague and had flown to South Africa for treatment. As you know, Robert has a passion for armoured personnel carriers, similar to Sam Nujoma's obsession with executive jets, and he has been diverting funds from the health budget for the purchase of large numbers of these vehicles. The result is that Zimbabwe has nothing more than a couple of packets of aspirin with which to treat dreadful diseases.

Naturally we immediately began phoning around hospitals and

health clinics in South Africa, to try and locate him. But none of them had any record of a Mr Mugabe in their beds, although there was one McCabe in an Upington clinic who denied emphatically that he was the president of anything.

Well, you can imagine the panic! I mean, he only had to bite a few people on the leg and we could have had the South African population succumbing to the Black Death. Police and troops were called off routine duties and a massive president-hunt was launched.

He was eventually discovered on Muizenberg beach. He was busily putting on a pair of water-wings when he saw the health inspectors coming for him, dressed up in protective overalls and gas masks. Apparently he made a terrible fuss, screaming "I didn't know it was a whites-only beach, I promise you I didn't know ...!!" They had to shoot him with a narcotic dart borrowed from the Parks Board and then rushed him off to a top secret chemical weapons laboratory where, after extensive tests, it was established he had a slight case of sunburn, but no traces of the bubonic plague.

He was hurriedly taken back to Muizenberg, still asleep, and dumped on the beach. Latest reports from Harare say he told Zimbabwean state television on his return that he had enjoyed a wonderful holiday in Cape Town, so hopefully he thought it was all just a bad dream.

I thought the Bloemfontein conference went off quite well. We did have some trouble from the press, complaining at the fact that it all took place behind closed doors — going on endlessly about ANC promises of transparency.

What they fail to appreciate is the sensitivity of the great matters of state we had to debate — the most important one being the question of what has happened to all the ANC's money. The trouble is someone has lost the books as well as the money, so we don't even know how much we had, much less where it has gone. Cyril has been muttering darkly about R70-million. Which makes me think we should have a closer look at where Elna Boesak got the funds to try and buy United Nations headquarters as the New York base for her video production company.

Winnie is insistent she will rescue us all from penury. For some time now the granny-of-the-nation has been acting very mysteriously, disappearing for long periods into Angola equipped only with a hammer and a chisel and that look in her eyes that means she is into another of her money-making schemes.

It turns out that her old friend, President Eduardo dos Santos, has his own diamond mine. Of course, because he is President-for-Eternity, or at least President-Until-Jonas-Savimbi-Is-Found, he can do what he likes with his diamonds. But lesser mortals are subject to international law as framed by Harry Oppenheimer which says that anyone found in possession of a rough diamond will be subject to frightful penalties.

Winnie consulted Mr Justice Albie Sachs about this. Albie has been digging his old law books out from the back of his aunt's chicken-run following his appointment to the Constitutional Court. After much patient work separating pages glued together by poultry fertiliser he discovered that a "rough diamond" is any diamond which is not a "cut diamond". So Winnie has been spending all of her spare time down Eduardo's diamond mine, banging away with her chisel and hammer at any pebble she can find, in the hopes of legitimating it.

She says the ANC can have the proceeds. That's after deductions for the various IDB operators who set her on the path to riches by donating their spare houses to her over the years. And, of course, after she has chosen the best specimens for the crown jewels she will have to wear at her coronation in Harlem next year as Queen of Africa.

I'm not sure whether there will be much left over to help the ANC. But anyway, looking at the shattered fragments she has been bringing back from Angola, I suspect Eduardo's diamond mine is in fact nothing more than an abandoned, underground bottle-bank. Either that, or Stompie must have ended his life with a rougher few hours than I appreciated.

Take care, old friend,
Nelson

1995

There was uproar in South Africa early in the New Year with the discovery that 3 500 members of the security forces had secretly applied for indemnity for crimes — which they did not specify — committed during the apartheid era. The indemnities had been quietly gazetted by the National Party government shortly before the 1994 majority-rule elections without anyone noticing.

Dali Mpofu was Winnie's young lawyer and lover. Albie Sachs had nearly failed to get his appointment to the Constitutional Court after admitting that — as a member of an ANC tribunal set up to investigate circumstances surrounding the mysterious death of an Umkhonto weSizwe guerrilla commander in exile — he had supported a whitewash finding for the sake of unanimity. Some members of the Judicial Service Commission felt unanimity was shaky grounds for a judicial decision.

Tokyo Sexwale, the Premier of Gauteng, who had boasted that he belonged to the propertyless classes, admitted his wife owned three flats in Johannesburg. Joe Modise, Defence Minister and former commander of Umkhonto weSizwe, had denied knowing that torture was routine in the ANC's notorious Quattro camp in Angola.

Nthato Motlana, Nelson Mandela's personal physician, became one of South Africa's wealthiest black citizens by urging wealthy whites to donate part of their ill-gotten gains to him in the name of black empowerment.

It was also reported that a number of persons jailed for indulging in the popular Australian pastime euphemistically known as "sheepshagging" had successfully petitioned for amnesty on grounds of political conscience.

The recently deceased South African Communist Party chief, Joe Slovo, was famous for his red socks.

OFFICE OF THE PRESIDENT

January 18 1995

Dear Walter,

We're having a terrible time with the Nats over this business about indemnity against prosecution. You will no doubt have read about it. It all started when Dullah Omar opened his lunch box and found, squeezed under his cheese sandwiches, a sheet of paper with very tiny handwriting on it. With the help of a microscope borrowed from the Human Sciences Research Council, he managed to establish that it was a government proclamation, dated April 24 1994, announcing the names of thousands of people who had been granted indemnity against prosecution for crimes they did not commit.

Dullah immediately called in General Johan van der Merwe, to demand to know what it was all about. The general said that the list had been put in the lunch box on the minister's first day in office and he could not be blamed if the minister was so preoccupied with his cheese sandwiches that he had failed to see it all this time.

He said they had had to fit all the names on one piece of paper because of a government stationery shortage at the time, resulting from the emergency printing of ballot papers to meet Gatsha's demands that all members of Inkatha be allowed to vote 50 times to make up for the elections in which they had not been allowed to vote.

He said they had put the list in the minister's lunch box on the assumption that it was the communist and terrorist equivalent to a ministerial dispatch box.

And he said that if the minister did not believe his story it was the minister's tough luck, because if the minister cared to look through his microscope again the proclamation specifically forgave the Commissioner of Police for hiding government proclamations from the minister — even though the allegation did not have a shred of truth in it and was part of the total onslaught aimed at discrediting that fine body of men, the security police, who did not

57

exist and who were anyway forgiven for all the people they tortured and murdered even though they didn't.

Of course Dullah came running into my office and I had to spend hours peering through this damned microscope. If you could read this document you would understand why my eyes have started weeping again. Quite apart from the 3 500 police they have indemnified for everything they did not do ranging from high treason to expectorating on the Blue Train, they have also forgiven Richard Nixon for selling second-hand cars he did not own and Paul Kruger for amputating his own thumb without appropriate medical qualifications.

The biggest entries were inevitably for members of the Cabinet under PW and FW. Vlok asks forgiveness for blowing up Khotso House and for criminally slandering Shirley Gunn — who, he had told the press, had done it — because anyone could have a minor lapse of memory about one's attempts to blow up the country's religious leaders and anyway what was someone doing with a name like Shirley Gunn if they did not have criminal intentions in the first place? Magnus Malan asks forgiveness for allowing the South African Defence Force to drive on the wrong side of the road on their way to conquer Luanda in 1974.

Of course when word began to circulate in the ANC about the indemnity proclamation a stampede started. I can see them through my window as I write, queuing up outside Dullah's door.

Winnie is at the head of the queue pushing a wheelbarrow piled high with confessions, Dali Mpofu sitting on the top to prevent them blowing away in the wind. Allan Boesak is there in his dog collar, carrying what looks like an alms box with a bust lock.

Albie Sachs in a judge's wig is waving his arm and shouting at anyone who will listen that he only found Thami Zulu guilty for the sake of unanimity and that was what democracy was about, wasn't it? Tokyo Sexwale is clutching the deeds of blocks of flats he does not own. Joe Modise is wearing the dark glasses that prevented him seeing what was going on at Quattro. And so the line stretches on ... Thabo and Sol Kerzner looking mournful, standing together ... several men displaying undue affection for the sheep accompanying them ... Motlana, R100 notes spilling out of his pockets, roaming up and down the queue, exhorting everyone to hand over their ill-gotten gains to him for conscience's sake ...

At the back is a flickering figure who is trying to light a piece of blue touch-paper sticking out of a barrel. He seems to be dressed up as Guy Fawkes. If I believed in ghosts I would have sworn he was wearing red socks.

With best wishes,
Nelson

*T**he** Polish dwarf and illusionist, Jarusvalskei, flits mysteriously
through the Dear Walter Papers. At a later stage the President
became convinced he was posing as the Deputy President,
Thabo Mbeki.*

*In pursuit of red mercury, investigative reporters at the Argus
newspaper group working in tandem with researchers from the British
television network, Channel 4, claimed they had established that
right-wing extremists had possession of one or more nuclear devices.
They also claimed another scoop when they reported that a South
African Airways jumbo, the* Helderberg — *which crashed off
Mauritius in November 1987, killing all 159 passengers and crew on
board — had suffered a previous accident on its ill-fated flight which
was covered up by the subsequent board of inquiry.*

OFFICE OF THE PRESIDENT

February 3 1995

Dear Walter,
It was a great relief to get back to the Union Buildings from India to
find peace and harmony on all sides. Winnie had disappeared on
some mysterious expedition which — to judge from the line of
porters who accompanied her, staggering under loads of pickaxes
and the like — no doubt heralds the discovery of new diamond
fields in Africa. Gatsha was busy down in Natal, devising some new
way of tormenting his King. And, much to everyone's relief, the
National Intelligence Agency had succeeded with the help of a
theodolite in establishing that FW de Klerk was indeed FW de
Klerk and not, as had been widely feared, a Polish dwarf and illusionist called Jarusvalskei.

I was just settling back behind my desk, planning a letter to my
old friend, Elizabeth Taylor, and thinking the cares of high office
were not so bad after all when a most frightening noise started.

It was the sirens of the nuclear-defence early warning system. Security men came rushing into my office, bundled me into an armoured car, rushed me to the government's top secret nuclear bunker under Ammunition Hill and whisked me into the underground Cabinet crisis room where my ministers were already assembled. Gerwel announced that the country's newly appointed spy chiefs, Sizakele Sigxashe and Mike Louw, would shortly be arriving to brief us on the crisis.

A few minutes later the door burst open and the two men rushed in, waving their arms excitedly in the air and shouting incoherently into the gas masks they were wearing. After Cabinet ministers had wrestled them to the ground and managed to tear the gas masks off the full story came tumbling out.

You will have read in the papers, Walter, that I have reorganised the Intelligence services into the NIA (National Intelligence Agency) and the SASS (South African Secret Service). Those, of course, are the agencies under government control.

There is, however, an even more powerful agency, in private hands. It is called the AIU, the Argus Investigative Unit. It was set up by the Irish fugitive, Tony O'Reilly, and as a result enjoys the formidable resources of all 57 Heinz varieties including their incomparable tomato sauce. This is the crack team of fearless investigators responsible for the greatest intelligence coup of the new South Africa — the recent disclosure that the *SA Helderberg* crashed several times before reaching Mauritius and that the Board of Inquiry covered up this salient fact by referring in its report only to "the crash" without disclosing to which crash they referred.

Well, it transpires that these investigative reporters have scored an even greater coup. Teaming up with a British agency so secret that it is known only by the mysterious cypher "Channel 4", they have been pursuing investigations into that terrible substance, red mercury, with which Russian scientists were just about to create atomic bombs disguised as ball-point pens when the Soviet Empire collapsed. In the course of these investigations the AIU and Channel 4 stumbled across a terrible South African nuclear secret: the right wing have got their hands on a nuclear bomb!!!

You can imagine the pandemonium that this announcement

caused in the Cabinet crisis room. Joe Modise was the most excited, shouting at Jay Naidoo that if he had let him buy the corvettes instead of wasting all that money on the RDP he could have wiped out the AWB with a swift and ruthless naval strike against Ventersdorp. It took Jay some time and the help of several maps to persuade Joe that Ventersdorp was not in fact a heavily fortified Indian Ocean island. Joe finally fell silent at this discovery, developing a contemplative look which I fear bodes ill for the future of the navy as South Africa's senior service.

After several hours of anxious discussion it was decided that Mufamadi is to order police to round up all bearded men wearing green underpants and carrying ball-point pens. I appreciate that this comes dangerously close to breaching provisions in our charter of human rights guaranteeing citizens protection against cruel and degrading treatment, not to mention the universal right of bearded men to carry ball-point pens and wear green underpants. But extreme crises demand extreme measures.

In the meantime we are confined to this bunker, waiting for the big bang. Wrap up warmly, old friend. The nuclear winter may be about to hit us.

With best wishes,
Nelson

arly in February police announced they were investigating a complaint by Archbishop Desmond Tutu that several hundred thousand rand donated by the singer, Paul Simon, to a South African children's charity had vanished. The charity — the Foundation for Peace and Justice — was headed by Allan Boesak and one Freddy Steenkamp.

This followed allegations by a Danish donor agency, Danchurch Aid, that Boesak had ripped off millions donated to the victims of apartheid by Denmark, Sweden and Norway.

The South African National Defence Force reported at this time that the high number of pregnancies among its personnel was posing a threat to the efficiency of the armed forces.

OFFICE OF THE PRESIDENT

February 10 1995

Dear Walter,

I must say nuclear bunkers have their uses. As I mentioned in my last letter, we took up our positions here, underneath Ammunition Hill, following the shocking discovery by our secret services that Tony O'Reilly's Intelligence agency, *The Star's* Special Investigations Unit, had discovered that a right-wing fanatic in green underpants was wandering about with an atom bomb disguised as a ball-point pen.

Since then I have been sequestered here with the Cabinet, in our underground crisis room, anxiously perusing the pages of *The Star* as it is rushed to us every day in the hopes of discovering fresh information on the looming Armageddon.

There was some excitement when a small item was discovered in the classified advertisements, in which an "Afrikaans poppy" offers to "tickle you pink". Analysts from the National Intelligence Agency speculated that this might be a carefully camouflaged threat by a right-wing anti-communist fanatic to blow the country up. But when one of our secret agents telephoned the number given he was made offers I will not detail in print, except to say they involved the use of a series of devices, none of which appeared to amount to an atomic bomb.

But even if the nuclear holocaust has not yet arrived we all have reason to be thankful that we are here, isolated from the daily explosions which constitute political life in our beloved country. Which is not to say we are completely out of touch, I hasten to say. We do get occasional communiqués from the battlefields outside, not to mention telegrams from the courageous folk who have chosen to risk all in order to keep the wheels of society turning.

I have a sheaf of them in front of me as I write. Admittedly some of them are fairly cryptic. On the top of the pile, for example is one from our soon-to-be-departed Commissioner of Police, General Johan van der Merwe: "CANCEL TRUTH COMMISSION, OR SWISS BANK NUMBERS WILL BE CHANGED." For some reason this greatly excited National Party Cabinet ministers who rushed out of the bunker, Pik Botha shouting that he had forgotten to tank up his car before the next review of petrol prices.

There is a loving telegram from Winnie saying simply: "HAVE SECURED SHOW BUSINESS MONOPOLY FOR ZINZI WHITNEY PROMISES MILLIONS KISSES." I'm not sure I am in need of millions of kisses from Whitney, whoever she may be, but it does show what a thoughtful mother Winnie is. She is a great believer in board games to keep the family together.

Here is one from Archbishop Desmond Tutu: "PRAYING ANC GETS OFF GRAVY TRAIN TO GENEVA AND GIVES KIDS THEIR MONEY BACK." Coincidentally, there are a couple more telegrams from another churchman, the Rev Allan Boesak who, as you know, I am sending to the United Nations in Geneva in recognition of the gallant efforts he made in the bad old days of apartheid to get me out of Pollsmoor Prison.

He's a wonderful speaker, Allan, but I must say his writing lacks the rich cadences of Martin Luther King which are familiar to his oratory. The first telegram we received from him says: "HELP". We subsequently received a longer, explanatory message from him which says: "FREDDY STEENKAMP DID IT." Strangely, both telegrams have the Pollsmoor Prison censor's stamp in the top right-hand corner.

There is a light-hearted message addressed to Joe Modise from Ronnie Kasrils who, with the courage to be expected of a highly trained Ninja man, has chosen to stay outside with his troops: "SOUTH AFRICAN NATIONAL DEFENCE FORCE PREGNANT AM TRADING CORVETTES FOR CONDOMS FOR SAKE OF RDP."

So, as you see, all is well with the country, at least to the extent that my government is able to discover what is happening in it. If only we had a window or two in this bunker. Modise has been trying to get hold of a periscope to put in the roof, so that we can at least have an occasional peep. But the only response he has had is a telegram from his admirals: "FOR SAKE OF POSTERITY ARE OBSERVING PENDING NUCLEAR HOLOCAUST UNDER ARCTIC CAP PERISCOPES NEEDED."

So if you hear a big bang, Walter, send me a telegram. It would be nice to know what is going on out there.

Best wishes,

Nelson

R elations between the Mandelas began to deteriorate early in the year. In February the President found himself battling to persuade 11 executive members of the ANC Women's League to withdraw their resignations. They were protesting against a deal struck by Winnie Mandela, on behalf of the League, with film star Omar Sharif to establish a joint venture called "Road to Freedom Tourists". The project was intended to make oodles of money by bringing African-Americans out to South Africa, to visit such landmarks of the liberation struggle as Mr Mandela's birthplace and his cell on Robben Island.

Other scandals involving Mrs Mandela abounded at this time, including allegations that she had misappropriated monies donated to South African charities by Pakistan Prime Minister Benazir Bhutto. Mrs Mandela, a great believer in the principle that the best means of defence is attack, chose the funeral of a black policeman in Soweto to deliver a blistering broadside against the ANC over its alleged failure to deal with racism in the new South Africa.

OFFICE OF THE PRESIDENT

February 17 1995

Dear Walter,

Valentine's Day and once again no sign of a card. Perhaps you think I am being unreasonable, but I must confess I was hoping to get one from her. I really had no choice, Walter. You should have heard what she said at that funeral!

Shakespeare is to blame. It all started at a cocktail party when someone made a reference to Shakespeare and Winnie said she had been introduced to him by her old friend, Whitney Houston. Of course this earned a raised eyebrow. The next day she was poring over her much-thumbed edition of the *International Who's Who* when Gatsha walked in. It turned out that he knew all about Shakespeare, having read up on him in order to pen his customary 15-page letter to some overseas newspaper, denouncing their correspondent as a liar and a cheat and a sodomite for suggesting he had shamed the Brutus tradition by his incompetent attempts to back-stab King Goodwill. Elucidated, Winnie dispatched Thabo — who is very good at running errands — to get a *Complete Works.*

Gatsha's contemptuous assessment of Brutus' handiwork where Caesar was concerned prompted her to turn to *Julius Caesar.* She was seemingly much taken by Mark Antony's famous oration, because the next thing she was shouting at her private secretary to find out if there were any funerals going on. When she heard that an unfortunate policeman was being buried — the one who made the fundamental mistake of holding his hands up in the air when he saw a member of the riot squad appearing over the horizon — she went charging off to Soweto.

My account of what then happened is secondhand, but appears reliable. Clutching her copy of the *Complete Works,* she rushed through the large crowd of mourners, shouldering aside the cleric who was just winding up a passionate sermon on the theme "render unto Caesar". Taking a deep breath, she announced: "I have come to bury Nelson, not to praise him." According to my informant, she then hesitated, glanced down at her *Complete Works,* muttered "silly bugger" and tossed aside the volume, which dealt a blow to the head of the poor cleric as he was trying to clamber back out of the grave.

Abandoning any pretence at blank verse, she proceeded to harangue the mourners with a tearful account of how she had sacri-ficed everything for the people, with the sole and perfectly natural exception of a lusty love life, only to be blocked and frustrated on every front by the well-known traitors in the ANC. By the time she had finished she had the entire crowd toyi-toyiing and baying for our blood, numbers of them falling into the grave in their excite-ment and squashing flat the unfortunate cleric.

Word, of course, quickly got back to the Union Buildings by the usual channels. By the time the ANC ministers had finished studying the CIA's satellite pictures of the spreading riot they were in a state of sheer panic and were soon banging on my door *en masse,* shouting for my keys to the nuclear bunker. I managed to calm them down and we were in the midst of a crisis meeting when a secretary rushed in to announce that a flushed Winnie had been seen returning to her office.

On the near-unanimous vote of the meeting, Thabo was thereupon dispatched to demand a written apology from her. He returned
a few minutes later with swellings to both eyes, explaining it was
due to the high pollen count. After threats to reduce him to Second
Deputy President he reluctantly headed off again, returning after a
more prolonged absence covered in ink and clutching a much-
smudged letter of apology. A proposal by Dullah that it be subjected
to handwriting experts was quickly ruled out of order and the letter
was rushed off to the newspapers.

And Winnie? She has been holed up in her office, writing away.
For a while I had hopes she was working on a Valentine's card. But
Mike Louw, who has managed to slip a miniature camera through
her keyhole, says it is a play called *Winnie and Nelson.*

It is the tale of a beautiful young woman whose feckless husband
lands up in jail, leaving her to fend for herself and her starving children, in addition to a faithless young lover; who is ripped off by foreign aid agencies, not to mention the Prime Minister of Pakistan,
when she discovers that she is really the daughter of a paramount
chief and is about to be crowned the rightful Queen of Africa when
she meets a fossilised Omar Sharif while on a diamond-buying
expedition to Angola in the sinister company of IDB smugglers trying to take advantage of her innocence ...

Well, you know the sort of thing, Walter. Shakespeare does not
have a chance.

Best wishes,
Nelson

*T**ensions** between the Mandelas escalated when Winnie Mandela flew off to a film festival in Burkina Faso, in defiance of her husband. While she was away heavily armed police using dogs raided her Soweto home in search of documents relating to a corruption inquiry. She returned home and managed to persuade the courts that the search was illegal. Police had to return the seized documents.*

Mrs Mandela also embarrassed her husband by accusing him of drawing up a letter, for her to sign, apologising to him for her recent behaviour.

OFFICE OF THE PRESIDENT

March 8 1995

Dear Walter,

Winnie again! And what a week it has been!

If I remember correctly, when last I wrote she was holed up in a movie palace in Burkina Faso. Actually there was, for a while, some confusion about that, thanks to Parks.

Parks has never been very good at geography. It turns out he was labouring under the misapprehension that Burkina Faso was a five-star hotel on the outskirts of Washington DC. So when someone leaked to the press that Winnie had gone off to West Africa to watch movies he was busy denouncing it as a lie put about by certain unnamed parties to undermine the RDP, insisting that she was in fact in Washington on top secret government business.

He then decided to telephone Winnie herself, to point out to her that the best place to watch movies in America was in fact in California and to tell her about the latest Clint Eastwood movie he had seen at the drive-in on top of a mine dump outside Johannesburg.

After several tense exchanges with the US operator, who insisted there was no hotel called the The Burkina Faso listed in Washington, he began shouting that it was the President's wife he wanted to talk to. He was immediately put through to Pennsylvania Avenue.

I walked into his office just as he was having an even more heated exchange with someone called Hillary, demanding to know why she was masquerading as Winnie and shouting that it was racism of the worst kind to reserve a house for whites. I managed to pull the telephone out of the wall just before he caused the most serious diplomatic incident since De Klerk offered Nancy Reagan a lifetime's supply of Durban Poison in exchange for the secrets of the neutron bomb.

When I had calmed him down and given him a quick geography lesson, Parks started hurriedly telephoning the press, to explain that he had of course been teasing and that Winnie was in fact in West Africa, staying at the five-star Burkina Faso Hotel in Washington. I, meanwhile, was left trying to figure out how to get her back to South Africa before the press started asking difficult questions about who gave her permission to go and watch movies in West Africa.

Fortunately, or unfortunately, she came back under her own steam — the phrase being something of an understatement in describing a phenomenon roughly comparable to the eruption of Mount Vesuvius. What had triggered her wrath was the news which had somehow reached the Burkina Faso bughouse, where she was watching a Clint Eastwood retrospective, that police had raided her palace in Soweto.

It transpired that, without my knowledge, the police were engaged in an investigation into allegations of fraud against Winnie made by some highly reliable witness serving a 99-year sentence for perjury, rape, murder, serial granny-bashing and conspiracy to commit armed robbery on a church alms box.

In pursuit of their investigations into this man's shock disclosures they had decided to raid her home. Being the fraud squad they carried out the operation with the care, logic and precision to be expected of trained accountants — laying down a mortar barrage before storming the house with a pack of rabid police dogs.

Inside the house piles of documents were discovered which the slavering dogs — having lived in a state of semi-starvation since the repeal of the pass laws — fell upon with gusto. The officer commanding the fraud squad, who had once seen an invoice while on a holiday in Pofadder and was therefore more knowledgeable about these things than his colleagues, realised they might contain a clue and belatedly gave orders that the documents be gathered up. This was done, five officers being mauled to death in the process, and the surviving mush rushed off to the chief magistrate of Johannesburg who is a jigsaw puzzle enthusiast and whose wife recently purchased a hairdryer.

Winnie arrived back home and fell into a fearsome rage. As she explained to the teams of lawyers she immediately summoned to start Constitutional Court proceedings, the police had not only stolen irreplaceable letters from Benazir Bhutto, Paul Simon and Whitney Houston — reassuring her that the millions of dollars in charitable donations they had made would be well spent on a tiara for her coronation as Queen of Africa — but one of their mortars had landed on her tool shed, destroying her personal arsenal and detonating the cache of explosives she had been saving for the day she exercised her inalienable, democratic right to blow up the houses of Parliament.

Then she really turned vicious, Walter. Posing as a highly reliable source who asked not to be named, she tipped off *The Star* that I had been writing letters to myself to be signed by her. It's a lie, Walter. Well, sort of. It was only a card. I just wanted to save her the trouble. And anyway some things should be in the nature of a sacred confidence between a man and his wife.

You see, I did feel hurt when she failed to send me a Valentine. My mantelpiece looked so bare. Admittedly I did go a little over the top, addressing it to "My lord and master..."

Regards,
Nelson

In March President Mandela visited Denmark.

Katiza Cebekhulu was a star state witness in the case against Winnie Mandela with regard to the murder of the 14-year-old boy activist, "Stompie" Moeketsi. Cebekhulu disappeared before he could testify and turned up in a Zambian jail. It is believed he was kidnapped by the ANC to prevent him testifying as to her presence at the fatal assault on Stompie.

**ELSINORE HOTEL,
DENMARK**

March 17 1995

Dear Walter,

I'm freezing cold and wish I was back home. This a very uncomfortable establishment they have put me in; a medieval castle staffed by people in period costumes bearing tankards of ale and roaring "Ho ho ho" in an authentic sort of way. Despite all the jollity, the room service is terrible, the plumbing sounds like the Battle of Isandhlwana and the bugs appear not to have been fed for centuries.

All of this would be tolerable, were it not for the stream of ghosts which keep clanking, squeaking and gibbering their way through my room. You know I am not a superstitious man. But one night in this place will persuade you that there are more things in heaven and earth, Walter, than are dreamt of in your philosophy.

My room seems to be a veritable rallying place for them. Heaven knows how many more are crowding the battlements outside. In fact the only difference between their gathering here and ANC monster rallies at home is that at least at the rallies I get to do the talking. With this assembly I barely get a word in edgeways.

What is particularly peculiar is that some of them look familiar, in a ghostly sort of way, of course. There is one, for instance, resembling that tubby man who runs the Reserve Bank. He (or it) irritates me mightily by constantly wagging a finger at me and repeating: "Neither a borrower, nor a lender be, for loan oft loses both itself and friend and borrowing dulls the edge of husbandry."

Then there is one who in appearance is the spitting image of FW de Klerk. He keeps waving a knife in the air, which he refers to as "this bare bodkin", shouting "To be, or not to be — that is the question." I try to interrupt him, to point out that, judging by his incorporeal appearance, he isn't, anyway. But he just ignores me, raving on about the "insolence of office and the spurns that patient merit of the unworthy takes".

Another, seemingly garbed in monkey skins, bears an unfortunate resemblance to Gatsha. Leaping about the place, brandishing what appears to be a skull, he pauses now and then to declare with ghastly leer: "Though this be madness, yet there is method in it."

A youth clad in chains introduced himself as one Katiza Cebekhulu and declared: "But that I am forbid to tell the secrets of my prison house I could a tale unfold whose lightest word would harrow up thy soul, freeze thy young blood, make thy two eyes, like stars, start from their spheres, thy knotted and combined locks to part and each particular hair to stand on end like quills upon the fretful porpentine." But — he added, when I suggested it was the sort of story Richard Goldstone would like to hear — "this eternal blazon must not be to ears of flesh and blood".

He was followed by a boy, a mere child of some 14 years of age who looked as if he had been beaten around the head. "Be thou a spirit of health, or goblin damned?" I demanded of him. But he just looked doleful.

I pressed on. "O! Answer me. Let me not burst in ignorance, but tell why thy immature bones hearsed in death have burst their cerements; why the sepulchre, wherein we saw thee quietly in-turned, hath op'd his ponderous and marble jaws to cast thee up again?"

This seemed to get to him, because he waved me to a more removed ground, inside the bathroom. He then made as if to climb through the window. "Where wilt thou lead me? Speak. I'll go no further," I said, knowing that a 14-foot fall into a stinking moat lay below.

"Mark me," he said.

"I will," replied I.

Then it began to croak: "Foul deeds will rise, though all the earth o'erwhelm them, to men's eyes." He was clearly about to go on — to speak, no doubt, a sorry tale of lewdness and lust and frailty whose name is woman, not to mention things most horrible — when the cock crew, that is the trumpet to the morn. The apparition started, like a guilty thing, upon a fearful summons and faded straight away.

At last I could sleep, this ghoulish assembly over. And as I drifted off I heard a last ghostly voice whisper: "Now cracks a noble heart. Good night, sweet prince ..."

The last thought I had, as flights of angels sang me to my rest, was: something's rotten in the state of Denmark.

Yours as ever,

A very tired

Nelson

OFFICE OF THE PRESIDENT

March 22 1995

Dear Walter,

Just a hurried note. I am frantically busy, dancing attendance on the Queen. It really is a full-time occupation, dealing with the English. They are a very strange people.

She arrived on Sunday. But don't mention that to anybody. We all had to swear an undertaking under the British Official Secrets Act not to divulge this detail. It seems the English are very concerned to persuade the world that they still rule the seas. They offer as proof of this the fact that their sovereign travels abroad on board her own ship — the point being that it demonstrates their confidence as the world's greatest seafaring nation.

Unfortunately, being German herself, she does not share their confidence. In fact I discovered that she views the leaky old tub they have given her with signal disfavour, nursing the suspicion that it is part of a plot hatched by some madman called Tony Benn to sink the monarchy. She also gets seasick.

So she flew into DF Malan airport secretly on Sunday, to be met by Thabo who, as his handling of Winnie demonstrates, is very good at pretending people are not there. She was then smuggled in the bottom of a laundry basket by train to Simonstown and on board the royal yacht Britannia disguised as a fisherman's wife to the cheers of millions lining the hills.

On Monday morning she sailed triumphantly into Cape Town harbour, surrounded by the remnants of our navy with teams of frogmen lined up on deck, ready to fish the old dear out of the water if necessary. As it transpired the boat made it, but not before several of the crew had to be rescued — falling short as they hurled themselves with grappling irons at the jetty in frustrated attempts to moor.

Assuming that queens always acted with great solemnity I was a bit surprised when this one came spiralling down the gangplank in what appeared to be a spirited rendition of the hornpipe. I was about to greet her with a hearty slap on the back, a cry of "Hey and a ho, my jolly Jack Tar" and the offer of a nip of rum when I realised she was just battling to hang on to her hat in the south-easter. So I made do with a cheery "Welcome to South Africa, Your Majesty," a conversational gambit which was met with a withering stare. A hatchet-faced man dressed up like something out of a comic opera hissed in my ear that "one does not initiate conversations with the Queen".

Fortunately the awkward moment was forgotten with the introduction of Princess Rochelle Mtirara of the royal house of the Thembu, who is my new companion. The Queen's eyes lit up on discovering she was a princess and she proceeded to bombard her with excited questions as to whether she could ever love a pumpkin; whether she knew what fun could be had talking to plants; and whether she would like to meet her son, Charles.

We all moved on to Tuynhuys where I faced a bit of a problem. The Cabinet had had a whip around to buy her a present and with the proceeds Trevor Manuel had purchased from a Taiwanese street-hawker contact a fabulous brooch in the shape of a diamond, gold and ruby peacock made out of bottle-tops. The difficulty was how to present it to her, without initiating a conversation. I tried tossing it into the air a few times, whistling a little ditty, in the hope of attracting her attention and a "What's that?" — enabling me to reply with an explanation that it was a gift. All I earned was a disdainful glare. So I slipped the peacock back in my pocket, determining to post her a gift voucher.

Yesterday we had a church service for her. This was at the insistence of Tutu who was very excited about the Queen, explaining that she was the Anglican pope and he had to treat her well to gain brownie points in the hereafter. I doubt if he earned many. Things did not go smoothly. First of all, the choir he had hired turned out to be a marimba band and Her Majesty looked decidedly tight-lipped as they jived around the altar. Then he had made the error of inviting Frene Ginwala to read one of the lessons. Under the apparent misapprehension that she was addressing a political rally she delivered a harangue about the iniquities of previous governments, weeping as she begged the world's forgiveness for the crimes committed

76

by the honourable leader of the opposition and his jackbooted, murdering henchmen.

Tutu himself then took the stand and tried to smooth things over by calling for a round of applause for FW de Klerk, appealing to him to stand up on a chair so everyone could see him. Clapping petered out when the familiar bald head failed to bob up, leading to the realisation that the Deputy President was playing truant.

Somewhat unnerved by this, Tutu called for a round of applause for the Queen and then the Duke of Edinburgh and then me and was working his way through the ranks of the Cabinet when he realised from the frosty looks being directed at him from the royal pew that there was not great enthusiasm there for this new form of worship.

He concluded the service by toyi-toyiing his way up to the aisle — failing by his example to persuade the Queen into following suit — before begging her to lift a bedsheet off a box-shaped object awaiting them in the nave. Her Majesty, apparently presuming it was the long-awaited gift, whipped the cover off with her first show of enthusiasm. Revealed was a concrete plinth with a brass plaque on which were etched the words: "We should all become fully human — Desmond Tutu, 1979."

Our archbishop is now in chains on board the royal yacht Britannia. There are some things you just do not suggest to a queen.

Regards,
Nelson

Gerry Adams, president of Sinn Fein — political wing of the IRA — visited South Africa at about this time.

OFFICE OF THE PRESIDENT

June 23 1995

Dear Walter,

I once heard the world of spies described as a hall of mirrors. I do not know who was responsible for the observation, but I am beginning to understand what he, she, or it meant.

There has been a plague of the British variety of secret agents around recently, disguised in bowler hats, Union Jack waistcoats and introducing themselves with roars of laughter as "Filby". They then proceed to babble on about attempts by the IRA to buy out De Beers with their ill-gotten gains and the differences between Irish partition and the bantustan system. It all seems to relate to a visit by a Mr Gerry Adams with whom I met and had genial, happy, relaxed, friendly and very useful discussions in the spirit of give and take and in joint recognition of the importance to peace in the world of common humanity. Unfortunately he spoke with a funny accent and I did not understand a thing he said.

But, to come back to spies, it is of course particularly difficult to know what is going on in our own espionage agencies, with Joe Nhlanhla in charge. As I have told you before, Joe has not uttered a word for the last 25 years for fear of inadvertently letting slip some terrible secret to which he is privy. In times of great urgency, or crisis I do manage to have attenuated conversations with him, asking him questions to which he reluctantly replies by writing down the answers on a notepad he carries with him.

Unfortunately, being a veteran intelligence agent, Joe then feels duty bound to eat the note. This plays hell with his indigestion. After extended conversation with him he tends to lock himself in the nearest toilet for lengthy periods of time, emerging with an anguished look on his face. I have tried to persuade him to experiment with rice paper, but he becomes very indignant — belonging to the old school which regards rice paper as a sign of moral decline. He is very old-fashioned, our Joe. The other day I walked into his office to find him weeping copiously over a secret letter he was preparing to an agent, having inadvertently squirted the lemon juice into his eye while endeavouring to write in invisible ink according to a formula he had found in an old *Beano* comic.

Anyway, I had occasion earlier today to question Joe about some of his recent appointments to the National Intelligence Agency and the South African Secret Service. One is Dirk Coetzee. You will remember him — the former commander of the Vlakplaas assassination squad made up of a variety of pornographers, freelance burglars and unemployed gardeners who used to idle away their spare time by patriotically murdering various of our leading citizens. Joe became very agitated at my inquiry, scrawling copious notes explaining that after various vocational guidance tests Coetzee had been adjudged the man best qualified to take over the Department of Wet Affairs and its stocks of Bulgarian umbrellas.

I also tentatively mentioned the chief torturer at the Quattro detention camp who was rumoured to have obtained high office in the National Intelligence Agency. More frantic scrawling ensued, this time explaining that the man in question had been hired to hide around corners at Intelligence headquarters and spring out on unsuspecting new recruits, kicking them in the groin in an attempt to prepare them for the hardships that lie ahead in their chosen profession.

I then queried the appointment, as head of our Moscow Station, of a former security branch agent who gained his reputation as a guardian of liberty by spying on his colleagues in newspaper offices. But by this time Joe was apparently suffering from an overdose of notepaper and he fled, hiccupping, into my bathroom. At the time of writing he is still there, no doubt playing with the mirrors.

Keep warm, old friend,

Yours as ever,

Nelson

Representatives of 20 Afrikaner organisations met Nelson Mandela to discuss the formation of an ethnic homeland for them. They presented him with a springbok kaross at the meeting. The President reportedly indicated he was prepared to consider a referendum on the volkstaat issue.

OFFICE OF THE PRESIDENT

July 4 1995

Dear Walter,

I had a terrible nightmare last night. It followed a meeting with a group of Afrikaners. At least I think they were Afrikaners — that is the point I want to come to.

They arrived in mid-afternoon in an ox-wagon which they proceeded to dismantle at the bottom of the stairs at the Union Buildings, carrying it piece-by-piece to the top where they reassembled it. With much cracking of whips and bellowing of oaths at the oxen, they made their way down the corridor to my office where they began banging on the door and shouting that they had come to see the "big chief".

I opened the door and one of them thrust a flea-bitten springbok skin into my arms, announcing that this was a gift from "the *volk*" and they had come to smoke the peace pipe. Another, peeking behind my filing cabinet, inquired as to where I kept my wigwam and a third proffered me a bag — full, it transpired, of colourful trading beads — which he said was in exchange for Pretoria.

They then produced a large map of South Africa. There was not much in the way of topographic detail. There was a small stick-man drawn in one corner of the country with the words written next to it: "Mandela's hut." On the other side of the country was a similar stick-man, who also seemed to be clutching an assegai, beside whom was the legend: "Buthelezi's hut." The rest of the map was painted orange, blue and white with the inscription written across it: "*Volkstaat!!!*"

After lengthy discussion, during which they conceded another hut for Beyers Naude and a couple of luxury German vehicles for Allan Boesak, I made the offer to them of a referendum. "Let the people decide," I cried. "Let the *volk* speak."

In retrospect I may have been a little carried away by the scenes at the Rugby World Cup. When you have had 98% of the world's Afrikaner population gathered in a stadium and baying "Nelson ... Nelson ... Nelson ..." you naturally develop some presumptions about the way the people are going to decide. I mean, if they voted "yes" for a *volkstaat* that would be the end of Chester Williams out on the left wing and some sacrifices are too high, even for a *volkstater*, was the way I rationalised it. Be that as it may my guests seemed very happy with the offer and headed off, singing "We are marching to Pretoria".

I did not give it another thought until later in the evening when I settled down with my cup of hot chocolate and slippers in front of the fire and set to work on page four of *War and Peace*. I did not make much progress. Something was niggling me. Suddenly I realised what it was: How could we have a referendum for Afrikaners without knowing who they were? How could we define an Afrikaner?

Shortly afterwards I must have dozed off, because I found myself participating in an extraordinary event. It was a sitting of the Race Classification Board. I was the chairman of the board and several members of the Cabinet were fellow commissioners. In front of us was a stage upon which a number of figures were paraded.

First up was Ferdie Hartzenberg. He strode backwards and forward, pushing his stomach out and shouting "Jirre jong, jirre jong!" This performance was met by catcalls from my fellow commissioners, Mac Maharaj crying out: "The boerewors test! The boerewors test!" An official hurried up onto the stage and jammed a piece of boerewors in Mr Hartzenberg's hair. He was then ordered to bend forwards and burst into tears when the wors failed to fall out. He hurried off the stage to chants of "Other Coloured! Other Coloured!"

Next up was FW de Klerk in a safari suit whose bald pate caused much heated, scientific debate among my colleagues. Eventually a comb was jammed in his socks and he was made to dance the hornpipe, departing the stage to further jeers when it fell out.

He was followed by Eugene Terre'Blanche, who was greeted with shouts of "Take them off ... off ... off!" All was about to be revealed when, thankfully, I woke up.

Of course every nation has the right to self-determination, Walter. But do green underpants qualify one for nationhood?

Take care,

Nelson

In a dramatic gesture of reconciliation towards the "ancien regime" President Nelson Mandela invited the wives of past heads of state — men like the arch-racist, JG Strijdom, and the "architect" of apartheid, Hendrik Verwoerd — to join him for tea at his Pretoria home, Mahlamba Ndlopfu (previously known as "Libertas").

Mrs Betsie Verwoerd sent her apologies, explaining she was too frail to attend, but invited the President to drop in for a cup of tea if he was in the vicinity of her home at Oranje, a whites-only settlement in a remote area of the Northern Cape.

OFFICE OF THE PRESIDENT

July 31 1995

Dear Walter,

Rattling around the various houses which are put at my disposal as President of the RSA, I occasionally feel twinges of longing for a wife. I know you are prejudiced in this regard — believing, as you do, that wives are not made for me. So you will no doubt be pleased to hear that I have now been cured of this peculiar form of nostalgia once and for all.

I am not sure what got into me, but I recently decided to invite all the wives, widows and so on who had occupied the presidential mansions to join me for lunch. It would be nice, I felt, to have the old walls of Libertas echoing once again with girlish laughter. I accordingly instructed Parks to issue the invitations — cautioning him, however, to leave Marike de Klerk off the guest list. You will recall the difficulties I had getting that good lady out of Libertas when I became President; I was not prepared to run the risk of having to use tear-gas to flush her out once again.

Parks, unfortunately, is a trifle weak on history and is not the most diplomatic of souls. Bumping into Adelaide Tambo as she was leaving a jewellery shop in downtown Pretoria and vaguely remembering that OR had been a president, he promptly invited her along to join the festivities. We hurriedly had to extend the guest list to include wives and widows of presidents of the ANC. I immediately received furious telephone calls from Zeph Mothopeng's widow, Urbania, demanding to know what was wrong with the PAC, and from Rebecca Kotane threatening to tell all about what happened on a certain occasion in my irresponsible youth when I took her for a romantic walk along the banks of Wemmer Pan. We accordingly extended invitations to wives, widows and so on of presidents of the PAC and secretary-generals of the SACP, broadening it further to spouses of freedom fighters who ought to have been heads of state after Nontsikelelo Biko left an ominous message with the switchboard operator asking me to call her back. To top it all the press began ringing, demanding to know what about Marike, to which Parks replied injudiciously by saying that she was disqualified, because her husband was bald — after which we had to disconnect the presidential telephones.

The big day arrived and I was alerted to the arrival of the first guest by a commotion at the front gate. Looking out the window I saw a little old lady in a granny dress bashing one of my bodyguards over the head with an umbrella, shrieking: "What have you done to my house!" I hurried down to discover that it was JG Strijdom's widow whose fury had been triggered by the guard's attempts to explain that Libertas had gone and this was now Mahlamba Ndlopfu.

The old lady calmed down when she spotted me and, labouring under the misapprehension that I was her old garden boy, one "Moses", allowed me to lead her to the house while berating me for failing to prune the roses in the manner to which she had trained me. I left her wandering around the corridors of Libertas cooing: "Hendrik, it's Susan, Hendrik ..."

The other guests arrived shortly afterwards: Elize Botha masquerading as Pieter-Dirk Uys in a dress of bar-coasters made out of tribal beads. Rebecca Kotane, winking lasciviously whenever she caught my eye. Rica Hodgson introducing herself to Mrs Diederichs as the widow of "Bomber Jack", Marga replying mechanically that she was full of admiration for the boys on the border. Tienie Vorster babbling about the need for national reconciliation, starting nervously every time Mrs Biko muttered: "The past is very difficult to forget."

By the time I got them seated — Mrs Strijdom grumbling that she was not used to dining with the domestic staff and where was that nice man Moses's wife, anyway — I had discovered how PW developed that finger-wagging tic. As silence finally descended, broken only by contented slurping and guzzling at the butternut gnocchi, the mussel and lobster chowder, the chicken lattice and the strawberry *millefeuille*, I was left pondering that the new South Africa truly is a marvellous thing. But maybe, when I take up Betsie Verwoerd's kind invitation to have tea with her in Oranje, I will go disguised as the garden boy.

Yours, "the happy bachelor",
Nelson

Disclosures of several key appointments to the security services, arising from initial publication of an earlier letter among the Dear Walter Papers (June 23, above), caused consternation in the South African intelligence community. A journalist living in Johannesburg was identified as the leak and it was decided to put a top surveillance team on his track, in order to discover his source. The plan was dropped, however — presumably because there were insufficient false beards to go around.

Publication of the following letter also caused some excitement, among lawyers representing a secretive soft-drinks company. Claiming their client had world copyright on the phrase "Shhhhh... you know who", they threatened to sue — proving once and for all that lawyers, as well as the law, are predisposed to be asses.

OFFICE OF THE PRESIDENT

August 25 1995

Dear Walter,

Roll out the tumbrils. Refurbish the Old Synagogue. It is treason of which I write. That is to say I am in trouble with the South African Secret Service, better known as "Shhhhh... you know who."

Do you remember that letter I wrote, Walter, about the appointments to the Secret Service? When I mentioned that John Horrock — the former security branch spy who earned the nation's eternal gratitude by helping subvert the freedom of the press — had been rewarded by being appointed head of Moscow Station? Well it was the Horrock appointment that has caused all the trouble.

It all arose when I found an envelope slipped under my door which, when I opened it, contained an invitation to a surprise party in the "Star Chamber" on the 10th floor of the Concilium Building in Skinner Street, Pretoria. It seemed late for my birthday, but frankly I was feeling a bit lonely — all the members of my Cabinet being away doing intensive research for the RDP at various luxury hotels in exotic locations around the world.

So I strolled down to the Concilium Building at the designated hour, feeling a small thrill of excitement as I passed through the portals of the place where such glorious chapters in our nation's history had been planned as the invasion of the Seychelles and the bugging of PW's telephone.

I also felt a small thrill of nervousness as I made my way up the stairs (the lifts being out of order), half expecting at every corner to receive a painful blow from the former head torturer at Quattro concentration camp who, as I have recounted before, has been hired by our National Intelligence Agency to lurk around the Concilium Building, springing out at unexpected moments to kick new recruits in the groin in order to prepare them for the vicissitudes of interrogation in far-off lands.

I made it safely to the 10th floor, however, to be confronted by a succession of hand-scrawled signs saying "Star Chamber Birthday Party This Way", which led me through a labyrinth of corridors to a pair of yellow-wood doors. Hearing no sound of gaiety within I knocked and was bade enter by what sounded like the cousin of the speaking clock.

It was gloomy inside, but I could just make out about a dozen people gathered around a large table, all of whom were wearing balaclava helmets out of which sprouted, unconvincingly, false beards, wigs, flapping ears and large red noses. In solemn silence I was ushered to an empty seat at one end of the table. The figure at the other end then demanded in a bass voice — which I assumed was also false, his voice rising to a squeak by the end of the sentence: "What have you got to say?"

I of course replied: "About what?" Which seemed to discombobulate this personage, because, much to my alarm, he banged his head upon the table and burst into sobs, saying in a broken voice: "How could you do it? How could you name the head of Moscow Station? I haven't been so humiliated since being arrested by the CIO in 1987 for spying on the Harare conference on the plight of the child under apartheid."

Upon this the other mysterious figures gathered around him, patting him on the back, "tut-tutting" and murmuring "there, there

Joe" before leading him weeping out the door. I was left alone, pondering the question as to whether I had really heard the first words uttered by the great Joe Nhlanhla — better known as "Z" — since he took his fierce oath never to utter a sound for the sake of secrecy.

I did not even have the opportunity of explaining how I met Mr Horrock. It was at a state cocktail party. He stood out in the company, being dressed rather bizarrely in a bearskin overcoat with a fur hat. He introduced himself with a smirk — "My friends call me Smiley" — and added excitedly that he had just been made head of Moscow Station. I expressed my enthusiasm and inquired politely as to how long he had been a ticket collector. Well I can't help it, Walter, if these people will insist on talking in code.

Yours in secret,
Nelson

*I*n August President Nelson Mandela announced he was seeking a divorce from his wife, Winnie. The sheriff of the court, however, had difficulties finding her in Parliament to serve the summons.

OFFICE OF THE PRESIDENT

September 4 1995

Dear Walter,

I suppose I should have known better. The warning signs were there. Three lawyers dropped dead of heart attacks when I telephoned them to broach the subject. My legal adviser, Fink Haysom, was seen swimming out to sea in the direction of the Falkland Islands, hyperventilating into a rusty aqualung he had kept as a souvenir from his days in the navy.

As word spread the messengers of Johannesburg's courts resigned *en masse*. Judges of the Witwatersrand Division simultaneously recovered from collective amnesia, announcing they had just remembered they were lifelong members of the Freemasons and/or the Broederbond and were prematurely retiring on grounds of a conflict of interest with everything.

Suddenly I gained an insight into the feelings of that American pilot as he watched the mushroom cloud climbing over Hiroshima. A small step for man, a giant calamity for mankind. Yes, I had decided to divorce Winnie.

I do not know what drove me to it. No, that is not true. It was that siren song from Cape Town and the eye drops.

You are probably a stranger to the impulse, Walter, with Albertina warming your bed outside those brief periods when Parliament manages to find a quorum. But it is lonely at the top. I am a man. And power is a potent aphrodisiac. In fact ever since my announcement that I was separating from Winnie there has been a never-ending stream of divorcees and widows pounding at the door, offering me comfort in the form of broth, knitted bed-caps and their grandmothers' secret remedies for enlarged livers.

Sometimes I would see a trace of russet among the grey hairs; detect a twinkle behind the rheumy eyes and old passions would begin to stir. But inevitably she would sneeze and as I watched the dentures flying across the room I would sadly reflect that there is a time in life for everything and perhaps this was not it.

But the urge was re-awakened one night when Rochelle was busily squirting the drops into my eyes. As I was submitting to that lovely young woman's ministrations the words of Archbishop Tutu wafted beguilingly through my mind; how nice it would be to have an adoring wife to help me carry the burdens of high office, specifically my slippers.

Not, I hasten to say, that Rochelle herself was a target of these lascivious thoughts. Apart from anything else, as you know, she is my great grandniece twice removed and the Mandelas have enough problems without introducing webbed feet. But her gentle touch brought to mind the saying of Von Clausewitz (or was it Michael Jackson?) that "When you think you are past love, it is time for your last love and one enchanted evening, across a crowded room ..." The next morning I awoke with joy in my heart and a spring in my step, resolved to rage, rage against the dying of the light, to grasp the nettle and so on and so forth.

As I mentioned earlier, there was a general reluctance in the legal profession to help me grasp the nettle and I was finally forced to turn to Ayob who, as his previous dealings with Winnie demonstrate, is daft enough to try anything. After much mournful mumbling over his law books he announced that the key to the whole process was to serve a personal summons on the lady — this being an arcane practice which developed obscurely from the tradition in medieval England of dancing around the maypole.

The difficulties in carrying out this task were obvious and manifold. Fortunately, as President, I have some influence and prevailed on Steve Tshwete to loan me the Springbok 4x200 and 4x400 relay teams. He did try and foist an affirmative action squad on me, indicating with a nudge and a wink that they would get their national colours, but I made it clear that some tasks were too important to allow principle to get in the way.

The runners were duly stationed at strategic points around the parliamentary buildings. At the sound of the noon gun the first of them, clutching the required forms in his hand, sprang from his starter's blocks outside the entrance to the National Assembly and, travelling with the speed and grace of a greyhound, hurtled through its portals.

The corridors of Parliament are something of a labyrinth and we are still trying to find out what happened. The remains of two have been recovered.

Love shall overcome all.

Your determined friend,

Nelson

*A*s part of his determined effort to persuade South Africa to "let bygones be bygones", the President invited Percy Yutar, the former attorney general of the Transvaal who had prosecuted him in the Rivonia trial, to join him for lunch. Yutar, a sparrow-like figure, declared his adoration for Mandela and tried to persuade reporters at a press conference that his prosecution of the Rivonia case was widely misunderstood. "I just did my duty ..." he said.

OFFICE OF THE PRESIDENT

November 29 1995

Dear Walter,

Guess who I ran into the other day? Percy Yutar! You remember: the man at the Rivonia trial who insisted on playing with his toy guillotine throughout the proceedings, giving us meaningful looks as he chopped off the heads of matches?

Well, it transpired I had invited him to lunch. That is to say Parks, who has taken my recent statements about the need for forgiveness and national reconciliation a bit literally, invited him to lunch on my behalf. In fact I was just tippy-toeing my way to the kitchen through the hallowed halls of Mahlamba Ndlopfu — one wary eye alert for Mrs Kriel, who is very protective of the delicious cold chicken-wings sometimes to be found lurking in the back of the presidential fridge — when I was interrupted by a midget enveloped in Homburg hat and overcoat who came bounding up the stairs towards me chirping: "Nelson! My oldest friend! The saint! You blessed man! At last ...!" He then threw himself into my arms; or at least failed in the attempt, eventually compromising by embracing my left leg and bestowing a resounding kiss on my knee cap.

As you can imagine I was a little taken aback by this performance, at first fearing that this was one of those bailiffs frustrated with lean pickings at Winnie's palace come to confiscate my collection of Valentine cards in the hope of selling them for an outrageous profit to the Irish ketchup king. When the confusion had been sorted out I found myself sitting down to lunch with Dr Yutar. The encounter represented a moment I had long dreamed of; like you, no doubt, I whiled away many of those long hours on the Island dreaming up pithy things I was going to say to the Transvaal attorney general when, as I promised myself, I one day managed to corner him in some dark alley.

As it transpired I could not get a word in edgeways. The man babbled on non-stop: how his lips were finally unsealed and it was all a case of mistaken identity he had never realised it was the same Nelson Mandela and if he had known at the time he would never have made those unfortunate remarks about the need to bring back drawing and quartering and boiling oil and besides did I know that on the night of February 10 1990 he had made a passionate appeal for my release to FW de Klerk who unfortunately failed to answer the telephone and ...

To make it worse, while mesmerising me with this torrent of words he managed to devour the three chicken-wings Mrs Kriel had reluctantly laid out for us. Finishing with a burp and a final chirp he slapped me on the back, apologised for having to rush and, with a whispered offer of help if I wanted to see Magnus and the boys strung up, flew out of the room. As I sat there, nibbling morosely on the few grains of rice he had overlooked, the thought suddenly struck me: I don't have to stand for this! Do I ? After all, I am President! Aren't I?

Galvanised by the thought I resumed my interrupted journey to the presidential fridge, seized a piece of cold sausage which had previously been obscured by the chicken-wings and made my triumphant way up to my study — narrowly evading a last-minute tackle by Mrs Kriel who had been hiding behind the Ming vase in the hallway.

Safe in my den I sat down and composed a letter to FW de Klerk, denouncing him as a Van der Merwe joke and inviting him to seek satisfaction if he considered himself a man of honour.

Would you like to be my second ? The duel is set for dawn on Sunday at the Fountains: fisticuffs at one metre. I should land a couple of good blows. To heck with reconciliation. I just hope nobody accuses me of conducting a vendetta against the vertically challenged.

Yours as ever,

Your champion,

Nelson

In December the Cabinet announced that Thabo Mbeki was to head a committee tasked to oversee the "reorganisation of state assets" — a euphemism for privatisation. The unions reacted with fury to the privatisation proposals, accusing the ANC of "selling off the family silver".

OFFICE OF THE PRESIDENT

December 13 1995

Dear Walter,

The great debate is upon us. Or at least it is upon me. It descended with great abruptness early in the morning a couple of days ago, when I tottered out of bed and, as is my habit, made my way to the bathroom and the adjoining place to reassure myself as to my identity, the continued presence of my hair, the whereabouts of my dentures, the efficient functioning of the plumbing and the various other routine checks against the wear and tear to which mortal flesh is heir.

Imagine my surprise, at this intensely private time in one's day, to discover what appeared to be a corporate board meeting taking place in my toilet, attended by a group of grave-looking men in pinstriped, three-piece suits. Hastily snatching the rather garish nightcap knitted by Mrs Kriel off my head, and tucking my toes in their similarly knitted bed-socks under the Persian rug in the passageway, I tried to make my presence known with a discreet cough.

They seemed to be preoccupied with some event taking place inside the toilet bowl and I had to let forth a series of less discreet coughs before I gained their attention. I asked if I could help. "Waste-Easy (Pty) Ltd" grunted a fat man sporting a large gold fob watch whom I took to be the chairman. "How many times ?" demanded another sharply, gesturing towards the bowl before I could ask for further elucidation from the fat man. I confessed to "about twice", adding hurriedly at the sight of his disapproving face that it was "sometimes more, depending on the number of state

94

banquets". "Not good enough," snapped a third with the hatchet-face of a financial director. Upon which they all trooped off into the bathroom where they busied themselves with the workings of the plug-hole.

Somewhat taken aback by this mysterious infestation of the capitalist classes I abandoned all further thoughts of inspecting the presidential person and hastened back to my bedroom, to dress. Making my way down to the ground floor, passing several more board meetings on the way, I shouted for Parks. He came running out of a back room pursued by a little man equipped with a clip-board, a measuring tape and a stop-watch who appeared to be involved in some complex calculation relating to the length and frequency of Parks's stride.

"What's going on!?" I shouted.

Parks shrugged helplessly: "Privatisation, Mr President."

"Privatisation?!"

"The Deputy President (First Class)," he nodded.

Thabo, it transpired, had discovered The Way.

You may or may not believe it, Walter, but Thabo used to be a leading member of the secret, underground and very hush-hush South African Communist Party. Unfortunately some years ago Comrade Joe Slovo, concerned that it was so hush-hush that there was some doubt as to its existence, decided it was time the Party emerge from the proverbial cupboard and called upon its members to stand and be counted. Thabo, whose height usually necessitates his standing in company anyway, displayed a sudden aversion to being counted and hurriedly sat down. Ever since he has been trying to put as much distance as possible between himself and the said gathering, throwing himself into the arms of those whose first commandment is to count only oneself.

Anyway, with the passion of the newly converted, Thabo had decided that collective ownership is a mortal sin, Parks explained. He had therefore announced that in future nothing belonged to everybody. In order to give a lead by example the government would immediately flog all the family silver from Mahlamba Ndlopfu at hugely discounted prices to those in the know and contract out such as the presidential catering contract to the highest bidder.

As Parks concluded this sorry tale Mrs Kriel passed by, kicking and screaming on the shoulder of a burly bailiff. "She insisted on using the coffee grounds only once," shrugged Parks.

Aghast at this sudden turn-around in my life I staggered into the dining room for breakfast, only to be accosted by a burly waiter who snarled: "Money first!" Resignedly borrowing some from Parks, at what I can only describe as usurious rates, I morosely settled down at the dining table. Moodily sawing with plastic knife and fork at the sawdust sausage and cardboard toast I reflected on the famous line of the Immortal Poet (or someone like that): "The markets know the price of everything, but the value of nothing."

Yours in wealthy penury,

Nelson

1996

O leg Soskovets, Russia's First Deputy Prime Minister, visited South Africa in November 1995. At a banquet in his honour Deputy President Thabo Mbeki announced that the Russians had invited him to send a group of young South Africans to Moscow for training as cosmonauts. "We are very moved ... South Africa will be the first African country to have an astronaut in space," Mbeki said jubilantly. More than a year after first publication of this letter, South African government officials admitted the project had got bogged down in disagreements as to who would pay.

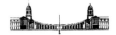

OFFICE OF THE PRESIDENT

January 1 1996

Dear Walter,
Happy New Year, old friend. I have not received your Xmas card yet, but one cannot demand too much of the postal services. No doubt I will stumble across it eventually, stuffed up some drainpipe.

I have been spending the festive season "on holiday" down at Qunu in the Transkei. Which means tramping around the countryside dogged by teams of drunken and quarrelsome journalists, working hard at "getting away from it all". The newspapers rhapsodise about the rustic charms of the Transkei, but frankly the place is full of terrifying memories for me: the big boulder I used to slide down as a child (the pain of it still lives with me); the trading store where I saw my first white people (now there's the stuff of nightmares) and the tranquil clearing where the mad axeman of Qunu performed my circumcision.

When I left the Island, in a fit of misplaced romanticism I ordered a house be built for me at Qunu. Some idiot of an architect, who obviously nurtured secret ambitions to be a stand-up comic, proceeded to design it as an exact replica of the house in the grounds of Victor Verster prison where I spent the latter years of my incarceration. I had to be dragged in, screaming and kicking, the first time I visited the place. Even now I cannot cross the threshold without a tremor, expecting at any moment to be traumatised by the sight of the best-selling author, Corporal Gregory, rooting around under my mattress in search of fresh material for another volume of his reminiscences.

But, as I chide myself, that is all of the past and it is the time of the year to be forward-looking. Which is a fairly terrifying exercise as well. The prospect of Tutu running the truth commission like a revivalist gathering, leading the country's killers and torturers in the toyi-toyi to the strains of *Onward Christian Soldiers,* is enough to make me wish I had never left Qunu. And then there is the space programme.

Have you heard about the space programme? I had my first inkling that something was going on when I spotted Thabo hanging upside down by his ankles from the statue of Louis Botha's horse at the front of the Union Buildings. A couple of days later I was nearly flattened by a 44-gallon drum rolling down the stairs of the amphitheatre. When it bounced to a halt at the bottom, out clambered a dishevelled-looking Deputy President (First Class). He finally exhausted my patience when he arrived at the year's-end Cabinet meeting with a goldfish bowl jammed over his head, upon which I demanded to know what was going on. We had to use a crowbar to get the bowl off his head before he could hear the question. Then, after various threats relating to the possible promotion of the Deputy President (Second Class), it all came tumbling out: Thabo was preparing to make space history.

It transpired that on a recent visit to South Africa the Deputy Prime Minister of Russia, one Oleg Soskovets, had let Thabo in on a bargain-basement, once-in-a-lifetime, never-to-be-repeated, all-inclusive special offer to take a trip to their Mir space station as Africa's first cosmonaut.

Somewhat wearily I inquired how much it would cost. After several mumbles, which forced me to recall FW de Klerk's unique leadership qualities, he confessed that a ticket was R93-million — adding hurriedly that that was business class and if we really wanted to be cheapskates there was an economy seat going for R43-million, but it only entitled one to a complimentary, dinky bottle of wine and plastic cutlery and besides one's luggage was the last to be unloaded.

I will draw a veil over the rest of the conversation except to say that he declined my offer of state funding for a one-way ticket and expressed his determination to raise the money himself for the greater glory of South Africa. Since then, I am told, he has been seen determinedly driving round and round Kyalami racetrack at high speed in what appears to be a Citi Golf rented from Avis. I haven't the heart to tell him that Mir does not qualify for air miles under the Voyager scheme.

With best wishes of the season,

Nelson

OFFICE OF THE PRESIDENT

January 24 1996

Dear Walter,

For a moment, I must admit, I was a little carried away. But, in the circumstances you can hardly blame me.

I was aching for a small change in diet from Tante Kriel's "koeksusters à la droewors". So when an invitation dropped on my desk to attend dinner with the leadership of the African Methodist Episcopalian Church on Saturday night I gladly accepted.

I had anticipated a quiet evening in the company of a few greybeards. Instead I walked into a gigantic hall packed with more than a thousand people excitedly dancing and writhing on the floor, waving chains, ringing slave bells and shouting hallelujahs. It transpired that these were the descendants — spiritual, if not genetic — of a group of 19th-century American slaves who, upon their manumission, had dedicated themselves to the cause of self-realisation with religious fervour.

This, it transpired, was the cause in which I have been labouring for much of my life — judging, at least, from the worshipful attention I received at the hands of Saturday's assembly. It was not just Bishop John Adams's reference to my "toughness of mind, greatness of spirit, everlasting patience and complete unselfishness", or Bishop Frederick C James's passing references to my "dignity beyond dimension, courage beyond contention". But then they started to refer to me as "the soaring symbol, the shining son, the ANC angel, the magnificent manifestation ..." I blush to go on.

You can imagine that this, coming on top of filet medallions topped with onion soubise and complemented by a sweet pepper and drambuie sauce with chocolate Bavarians, was a fairly rich diet. When I finally staggered out of the gathering with the words of Bishop John Adams ringing in my ears — "Your humility is such it does not allow you to understand how priceless you are" — I was in a pretty thoughtful state of mind.

By the time I made it back to Mahlamba Ndlopfu the question

loomed larger and larger: Was it possible ...? Could I be ...? I absent-mindedly said goodbye to my security detail and was trudging up the staircase to my room when the thought suddenly struck me: There was, after all, a simple test!

I hurried back downstairs and tippy-toed across the lawn. It was a moonless night and pitch-dark. After colliding with several of the garden gnomes that Marike de Klerk had declared national monuments before surrendering her precious Libertas to me, I finally made it to the small and shallow fishpond. Groping my way carefully I stepped over the edge. And I walked, Walter! Without so much as getting my shoes wet!!

You can imagine that I went to bed in a fairly disturbed state of mind. I mean, apart from the burden of responsibility, it posed certain questions of a personal nature. What effect would it have on my tax status, for instance? And would Winnie still be entitled to half my estate?

The next morning I was awakened by an anxious-looking Parks who said the polygraph man had arrived. By way of explanation a morning session with the lie-detector machine has now become obligatory for all security force commanders, Cabinet ministers and above to enable Mufamadi to keep track of all the fibs being told on a daily basis.

I hurried down to the Truth Room which has been set aside for this purpose and was duly strapped in by the operator who, as is customary in these sessions, opened by inquiring who I was. I told him. He gave a nervous laugh, slapped me on the back, looked at the machine and his mouth dropped open. A series of hurried questions followed relating to my father's occupation and the circumstances of my birth before the polygraph operator abandoned his machine and rushed babbling down the corridor.

Word spreads quickly. By the time I got back to my bedroom a crowd had overwhelmed the guards at the gate and was gathering on the lawn. I walked out on to my balcony to chants of "Show us! Show us!" Raising my arms to command silence, I had just begun to declaim "I am what I am ..." when to my horror I spotted the fishpond behind them. It was empty! I had forgotten that Kader had drained it as part of his drought relief programme.

What can I do, Walter? The people are expecting miracles.

Yours,

Nelson

The controversial American black Muslim leader, Louis Farrakhan, was granted a meeting with Mandela after some debate in the ANC. Farrakhan — the leader of the Nation of Islam who in the past had described Jews as "bloodsuckers", the Pope as a "no-good cracker" and supported a call to South Africa's blacks to butcher the whites — had just won the support of Moammar Gaddafi for plans to force the racial partition of the US and found a black state with "the biggest black army on the planet".

OFFICE OF THE PRESIDENT

January 30 1996

Dear Walter,

Do you remember Benny Alexander? The PAC leader with the eternal look of a schoolboy who has just been caught with his thumb in the plum pudding and is going to deny it no matter how much jam is smeared across his face? Like you, no doubt, I thought he had disappeared into obscurity with the rest of the PAC when they ran out of church-goers to massacre. It is not the case.

He popped up unexpectedly last week in the strangest circumstances. I was taking a break at my home in Houghton when I received a telephone call from an irate neighbour, complaining that there was a near-naked man leaping up and down outside my security wall, making funny noises and gesticulating with a bow and arrow. While appreciating, said the neighbour, that this was not the Court of St James, and that top hats and tails were not *de rigueur* for audiences with the head of state, would I kindly let the poor man in before he took a chill and frightened his (the neighbour's) daughters into Sapphic retreat?

I hurried down to the front entrance to discover the guards had gone for their tea break. Dragging the security door open I was startled to find myself confronted by Benny dressed in a loincloth. I recovered myself, and greeted him by his given name. Upon which

103

he whipped his bow from around his shoulder, menaced me with an arrow which appeared to have been dipped in plum jam and let out a series of shrill cries interrupted by clicks. Then, lowering his weapon, he said that as a sell-out to the capitalist classes I could not be expected to understand the true language of the people, but his name was now !Khoisan X and if I ever had the effrontery to call him by his slave name again he would not hesitate to plug me with his arrow which, he pointed out, was coated with a deadly poison made from a secret recipe for plum jam given to him by his grandmother on her deathbed against an anthill in the Great Karoo.

Somewhat taken aback by all this I invited him into the house and he followed, muttering something about the decadence of walls. I crouched down with him on the Persian rug in the sitting room and inquired how I could help. Upon which he whipped a piece of paper from a monkey-skin pouch tied around his waist and presented it to me with a dramatic flourish. It was a summons to meet someone called Louis Farrakhan at my house on Saturday.

Over the next couple of days I phoned around members of my Cabinet to try and discover who this gentleman was. The ministers I spoke to were not much help, because, as they explained, they had just remembered they were going on leave and did not have time to talk. I was eventually driven to having Nzo woken up, but when he heard Farrakhan's name he began shouting for his sleeping pills.

It was, therefore, with a degree of nervousness that I awaited this appointment. My nervousness was not abated when he arrived in two Soweto hearses. My neighbours, anxious to see who in the street had been claimed by the eternal reaper, crowded their second-storey windows. This strange man clambered out of his vehicle, waved his fist at them yelling "bloodsuckers" and, muttering something about "Wait until I tell my old friend Adolf", marched into my home.

With a cry of "Allahu Akhbar!" he presented me with a T-shirt bearing the mysterious slogan "Million Man March" and announced that in exchange he wanted a homeland for "the freedom-seeking slave children of the Americas". I started temporising, trying to point out that homelands were not in fashion in our part of the world, upon which he began shouting that it was their inalienable

right to claim their rightful inheritance in Africa; that their ances-
tors had been dragged off the continent without so much as a by-
your-leave much less a democratic vote and ...

Somewhat desperate I told him I did happen to know of some
under-utilised property on the banks of the Orange River. He left,
babbling excitedly to his delegation about a land of milk and honey
called Oranje.

If Betsie Verwoerd knew who is coming for dinner ...!

Yours,

Nelson

I n February a security guard slipped on a step at the President's
Cape Town offices, hurting his ankle. An ambulance was called.
The sight of the emergency vehicle at the presidency started another
round of endless rumours about Mandela's health, triggering a run on
the stock exchange.

Mandela also had to deal with a foreign affairs crisis at about
this time, precipitated by reports that an Algerian rebel leader, Anwar
Haddam of the Islamic Salvation Front, had been invited to meet
him.

OFFICE OF THE PRESIDENT

February 20 1996

Dear Walter,

I have been pondering the great issues of existence again.
Intimations of mortality, I suppose. Hardly surprising after recent
events. Did you read about the panic?

One of my guards ricks his back trying to load his bazooka and
an ambulance is summoned. The ambulance driver, who nurtures
secret ambitions to be Nigel Mansell, does a three-wheeled skid
outside the British High Commission. The local MI6 representative,
up a jacaranda tree in the High Commission's front garden — trying
out a new pair of binoculars his mother-in-law gave him on the
blonde Israeli second secretary who has a taste for skinny-dipping
— sees the said ambulance disappearing towards my house. He
rushes into the High Commission and sends a top secret, scrambled
message to the British foreign secretary, advising him to off-load his
shares in SA Breweries.

The CIA, Mossad, the Deuxième Bureau, the Tasmanian Secret
Service and the Swiss Association for Lost Persons Seeking
Anonymity intercept the message and pandemonium hits the money
markets. What's-his-name, the rotund man who claims to run the
Reserve Bank, says he would not think of interfering with market

forces and Diagonal Street promptly underlines the point by raining
stockbrokers. The panic spreads to New York, the dollar tumbling
yet further against the yen, stockbrokers bouncing all over Wall
Street, when I am woken by a pounding at the front door. It is a representative of the World Bank nervously clutching a "get-well" card.

It is getting out of hand. When someone greets me with a "How-
are-you-today-Mr-President?" the international money markets hold
their collective breath. Most people think the men clutching two-
way radios who surround me when I go walkabout are bodyguards.
In fact they are representatives of the world's leading merchant
banks who go into a state of hysteria whenever I sneeze. The other
day I had to give one of them cardiac massage after he had heard
me ask Parks for Tutu's telephone number. He thought I was asking
for the last rites. All I wanted to do was ask the good archbishop
where I should drop off my application for amnesty, in the light of
his reported finding as chairperson of the truth commission that "We
are all guilty".

I hope I am not sounding too maudlin, but this high office is tir-
ing. It is not so much cleaning up after Nzo and company —
although it is wearisome having to make these frantic calls to
Algeria, explaining that the only Anwar Haddam I had met was a
gentleman applying for the post of head waiter at the Groote Schuur
staff canteen — but the dramas attendant on diplomatic ceremony.

Earlier this week, for example, I was introduced to a sweet lady
who — thanks to an intermittent fault in one of my hearing aids — I
took to be a pastry cook. Priscilla slipped me a note explaining that
she was the Queen of Denmark which was famous for its pastry, but
that she was not a cook herself. I had only just recovered from this
faux pas when the Queen in question whipped what I took to be a
stale Danish bun out of her handbag and presented it to me. I was
about to risk my dentures on it and give the appropriate "yum, yum"
noises when I realised that what I had taken for a large raisin was in
fact a glass eye staring at me malevolently. On closer examination I
realised that it was an enamel and gold statue of an elephant. The
Pastry Queen thereupon announced to the assembled courtiers and
Groote Schuur gardeners that this was her country's highest award,
the Order of the Elephant, which represented chastity and purity.

I managed to delay proceeding by gabbling on about Betsie Verwoerd's secret recipes for koeksusters, giving Parks time to run into the kitchen and set about an empty baked-beans tin with the hammer and gold spray-paint which he keeps handy for such emergencies. I was thereby able to salvage national honour and proudly present her with our highest award, the glittering Order of Good Hope, Class 1, Grand Cross (Gold), sponsored by Heinz.

The Order of the Elephant! Chastity and purity!! I hope Winnie does not get to hear of it. She'll subpoena it for the divorce action.

Yours,

Nelson

T*he Minister of Health, Dr Nkosazana Zuma — one of three wives of the Natal ANC leader, Jacob Zuma — landed in the middle of a scandal over an Aids play called* Sarafina 2. *The production, which enjoyed little success, cost R14-million to stage — representing a goodly part of the government's budget to fight Aids. There were allegations of irresponsible spending. Dr Zuma tried to deflect criticism by claiming the money was donated by the European Union and the play would cost the South African taxpayer nothing. This was denied by the EU.*

OFFICE OF THE PRESIDENT

February 27 1996

Dear Walter,

There's no business like show business, goes the old refrain. I must say the point is borne out by Nkosazana Zuma's latest production.

How my Minister of Health got involved in the theatrical business in the first place remains a mystery to me. I had thought her busy in remote corners of the country, encouraging the blind to engage in bird-watching activities, the lame to pick up their beds and trot about the place, not to mention various other miracles consequent on free primary health care.

You can imagine my astonishment, therefore — driving into Tuynhuys to put in a few hours' work on the various crises arising from Nzo's peculiar approach to diplomacy — to see Cape Town's lamp-posts dressed in posters announcing the première of Nkosazana's "latest hit play", entitled *Aids! Aids! Aids!*.

When I got to the office I inquired of Priscilla whether I had an invitation, only to be told regretfully that seats had been sold out 10 days before and that, such was the high price of the tickets in the first place, the scalpers had all gone out of business.

Well, there are few perquisites of office remaining to the presidency in these days of austerity, but after much shouting and scurrying about I found myself seated in the gods at the Baxter Theatre enjoying — with the help of a periscope loaned to me by Modise — an uninterrupted view of the stage.

The sense of anticipation in the theatre was electric and was heightened when the orchestra played the opening bars of Beethoven's *Ninth*. They played them again and were hesitantly playing them a third time when one corner of the curtains was lifted and a man stepped through to be greeted by thunderous applause in the popular assumption that he was the hero of the piece.

This turned out to be premature, the character in question being the author, who had various complaints he wanted to get off his chest about the parsimony of government and the European Union as well as the high cost of insuring his new BMW.

The reference to the European Union seemed to trigger some indignation from the front row. A small man with a goatee who, it transpired, was the ambassador of the said union, clambered on to the stage and punched the distinguished author on the nose, shouting that it was a foul libel on his masters. The two set about each other and rolled off, stage left.

The silence which followed was broken by another tentative attempt at Beethoven's *Ninth*. To everyone's delight the curtains then flew open, disclosing a chorus line of 101 Cuban doctors who marched to and fro waving condoms over their heads and chanting: *"Hasta la revolución siempre!"*

I will not go into the detail on the rest of the performance; I am sure you will want to see it for yourself. Suffice to say the first act was devoted to long agonising between the heroine and the hero about whether they should do it or not. The second was devoted to long agonising between the hero and the heroine as to whether they should put one on before they did it. The production built up to a thrilling climax in the third act when they discovered there was a hole in it. Amidst scenes of great indignation suspicion inevitably falls on the US ambassador and the play ends with 101 Cuban doctors marching to and fro, chanting "Go home, Yankees".

The curtains fell to a standing ovation and cries of "Author! Author!" The author duly appeared, but failed to tarry. Clutching his BMW keys he hurdled over the heads of the orchestra and disappeared up the aisle, pursued by 101 Cuban doctors shouting demands that they be paid.

Then on to the stage stepped none other than my Minister of Health herself. Delivering a diatribe against promiscuity in general and polygamy in particular — against the latter of which she seemed to harbour a particular resentment — she appealed to the audience not to do it at all and, if they had to, to stick to all proprieties where the State Tender Board was concerned. This incisive approach to the greatest crisis of our times was received with another standing ovation and we all went home pondering what had been done with the rest of the R14-million.

Yours as ever,
Nelson

OFFICE OF THE PRESIDENT

March 6 1996

Dear Walter,

I am just back from Swaziland where I met the young King, Mswati. I must say that whenever I come across the world's surviving monarchs I cannot help but reflect that their lot in life is an unhappy one. You will recall I wrote to you before about some of the tribulations suffered by our own King Zwelithini — the ridicule which the virgins visited upon him on the occasion of last year's Reed Dance, jeering and waving broken straws at him. King Mswati's problems are slightly different.

I went to Swaziland on a secret mission to persuade the young man to allow at least one or two political parties to hold the occasional meeting in his country, as has been demanded by the local trade union movement. He got most upset when I tentatively broached the subject over lunch, breaking down and sobbing into his pumpkin soup. I tried to console him, murmuring platitudes about the relief of relinquishing the heavy burdens of office, but he only sobbed more loudly between mouthfuls of pumpkin fritters. Finally, when we moved on to the pumpkin mousse, the story came out between sobs.

You may recall that Mswati's father was King Sobhuza, who died a few years ago. One of his achievements in life was that he established a world record in wives — the precise number of which has been disputed, but looks something like a cricket score. Well, when the old man finally expired of exhaustion there was apparently quite a deathbed scene — the King lying there, surrounded by acres of weeping wives, a fading twinkle still in his eyes as he surveyed the heaving bosoms which were his lifetime's work. In kingly tradition he summoned his heir to deliver a few farewell words of advice. Raising himself on one elbow and gesturing at the host of grieving women, he gasped: "Keep up the good work, son" and passed away.

Mswati naturally took his father's dying words to heart. As you

know, every December as part of the *incwala* ceremony all the kingdom's most luscious virgins are paraded in front of their monarch for
his delectation. A nod of his head and the lucky girls are shown into
a back room of the royal kraal where a mysterious ceremony takes
place according to customs handed down from king to king —
details of which remain a jealously guarded state secret, but which
inevitably conclude with the said maidens emerging with a big
smile on their faces.

After consultations with his various viziers and sports coaches
Mswati subjected himself to a strict regimen of exercise and diet of
pumpkins, determined to do his best by the family name on this
field of battle. Remembering the good advice of Bob Woolmer, who
used to be his cricket coach at Sherborne College, the young King
decided that "slow and steady" was the best way to rack up a good
score — resisting the temptation to go for fours or sixes, making do
with quick singles. By dint of hard work and careful concentration
he had chalked up seven wives — which, you must admit, is not
bad at 28 years of age — when the clamour started for majority rule
and trade union rights.

I made the point to the King that this was perhaps no bad thing;
if he could relinquish the arduous duties of government he could
concentrate on the task at hand and more effectively devote himself
to the fulfilment of his father's wishes. But this innocent contribu-
tion had him choking on his after-dinner pumpkin seeds. He recovered to blurt out that his wives had on a majority vote declared
themselves a closed shop and had instituted a work to rule until
such time as he conceded a 40-hour week and overtime for duties
attended to outside office hours! How could he now fulfil his father's
wishes, he cried!?

I quietly made my excuses — explaining I had a few problems to
attend to in Mali and Togo — and departed the table. As I was
whisked away in my helicopter I had a last glimpse of the "Sire of
the Herd" moodily picking his teeth with a pumpkin stalk.

It is a high price some must pay for democracy.

Yours in happy bachelorhood,

Nelson

B ritish newspaper readers were kept agog by the race against time by a self-proclaimed Xhosa chief, Nicholas Gcaleka, to discover the skull of an illustrious ancestor, King Hintsa, killed by British colonial troops. The skull was reputed to have been taken back to the UK as a souvenir and to be languishing in an unidentified museum. Gcaleka claimed to have been visited in a dream by King Hintsa and warned to bring back the skull for burial before the anniversary of his death, or the local community would face disaster. Gcaleka returned in triumph with what he claimed was the skull, but forensic tests established it was that of a Caucasian woman. Subsequent to this letter, he was prosecuted for fraud.

OFFICE OF THE PRESIDENT

March 15 1996

Dear Walter,

I hope you have not been too concerned at recent reports about my health and hospitalisation. There were no immediate fears; I was just being prepared for the big event, like a boxer who has to undergo health checks in advance of a title bout. Yes, the moment of truth is almost upon us. The divorce looms.

"Relax, relax, relax," is the constant refrain from my advisers, ears cocked for the latest word from the opposition's training camp. By all accounts she is a new woman: fighting fit, muscles rippling, shiny new wig ...

The trouble is I find it extremely hard work to relax; the pressures on one as head of state are overwhelming. Take yesterday, for example. I was having a quiet snooze in a deck chair in the rose-garden at Genadendal — just getting to the point in my favourite dream where Winnie gratefully accepts a presidential pardon for eloping to Barbados with Brian Lara — when I was awakened by the most almighty caterwauling sound.

I leapt to my feet, convinced that the last trump had sounded, to be confronted by an awful apparition advancing across the lawn towards me: a man in a kilt with eyes popping as he endeavoured to give mouth-to-mouth resuscitation to what appeared to be a dying sheep tossed over his shoulder. With a final shriek from the unfortunate beastie this strange figure came to a halt, saluted me and announced that he was none other than Dougal Nicholas MacGcaleka of the fighting MacXhosa, great-great-grandson of King MacHintsa, the second cousin twice removed of Robert the Bruce who was foully done to death (MacHintsa, that is, not MacBruce) by the English on May 12, 167 years ago.

Fearful that this fearsome-looking fellow would follow this up by biting me on the ankle I hurried to reassure him that I was well aware of the glorious history of the fighting MacXhosa — modestly noting that as a MacDiba myself, albeit it through a junior house, I was to some extent an heir to the glorious tradition.

He acknowledged that it was the rumour of my royal lineage that had prompted him to seek me out. I bade him take a seat and offered him a cup of tea. He declined in favour of a plate of porridge and, putting his awful-smelling and now seemingly dead sheep to one side, proceeded to tell me a tale fit to chill one's very bones.

It all started one night late last year when this MacGcaleka was snoring away in his huts on the periphery of the Great Place in the Transkei, dreaming that he was Brian Lara. He had just got to the part where Lara was about to elope with Tina Turner when the broadcast was interrupted by a man who appeared much agitated — understandably so, as he had no head. By means of sign language this apparition signalled that he was King MacHintsa and that he was sick of wandering around in the hereafter in this sorry state. If his lazybones of a great-great-grandson did not stop his dreaming and get himself off to that land where men were men — and showed it by wearing skirts — to retrieve the missing item by May 12 he would visit the usual plagues of boils, locusts and more Winnie Mandelas on the local population.

To cut a long story short, after many adventures involving tabloid newspaper journalists he landed up in a boarding house in Edinburgh. The landlady of this establishment, much tickled by the discovery of what lay beneath his skirt, took him to her bosom in a manner of speaking and introduced him to the Scottish way of life, including the local religion which involved visiting local shrines and drinking an amber-coloured liquid which gave the worshipper sacred visions.

MacGcaleka consumed large quantities of this liquid, in the hope of conjuring up King MacHintsa again and getting a insider's tip on where to discover his missing head. Unfortunately his ancestor failed to make an appearance in the many visions he enjoyed. But he did fall into the company of a number of journalists who happened to frequent one of the shrines he visited and in the course of these religious rites they were able to guide him to a local cemetery where, to the accompaniment of much singing and shouting, they excavated a grave and found a skull. MacGcaleka was immediately able to identify it as that of his illustrious ancestor from the detail that it had no ears — it being well known in the Transkei that King MacHintsa was shorn of the said appendages when he was done to death by the English.

To cut another long story short, MacGcaleka returned home to make a triumphant appearance at the Great Place, brandishing the skull, sporran swinging and bagpipe wailing. This cause scenes of general consternation in the course of which, he recounted, the skull was marched off to Willowvale mortuary under armed guard and he only just escaped from the ...

At this point of his narrative MacGcaleka went rigid, his attention caught by the sight of an ambulance coming down the driveway to Genadendal. The next moment he was bounding over the rose bushes and through the hedges, hotly pursued by two men in white coats.

I wonder what is going to happen on May 12.
Nelson

Tthe long and troubled Mandela marriage finally came to an end at a two-day hearing in the supreme court presided over by the Judge President of the Transvaal, Mr Justice Eloff, and attended by the judge's wife who was allowed to take up a position on the press bench as a result of a misapprehension that she was the local correspondent of Penthouse magazine. Nelson Mandela was represented by a formidable Afrikaner "silk", Wim Trengove. Winnie Mandela fired her counsel midway through the hearing, but she failed to turn up for the second day's hearing.

OFFICE OF THE PRESIDENT

March 20 1996

Dear Walter,

Free at last, free at last; thank God Almighty I'm free at last. The gates breached, the battlements taken, the inhabitants put to the sword. Victory, glorious victory.

It's the roly-poly Greek I have to thank. You've no idea the panic in legal circles when Fink circulated word that I needed an advocate to help me divorce Winnie. Mass resignations from the Bar; a stampede on the passport office; petitions to the UN for refugee status ... I was getting desperate when I found a piece of paper pushed under my bedroom door with a message scrawled in George Bizos's unmistakable handwriting: "Get Wim."

I immediately summoned the human bloodhound, Joe Nhlanhla, and issued him with the order: "Get Wim."

"Wim?" he cried, a look of terror crossing his face. But he saw from the implacable look on my face that I would brook no half measures in the face of the enemy.

I believe the NIA lost five of their best men before they finally cornered the legend on his Harley Davidson in a remote part of the Kalahari. There, with the help of loud hailers, they managed to get the message across to him: "Your country needs you, Wim." I think

117

it was the challenge as much as the call to patriotic duty which persuaded him: there is, after all, only one Winnie. Thank heavens.

I came to understand the terror Wim inspires when he finally arrived at my Houghton home, hospitalising the doorman who had the temerity to ask who he was and burying two of my bodyguards under the petunias after they had made the mistake of trying to search his briefcase. He cut a fearsome figure; the popular description — "a balding skinhead" — does not do him justice. (He was later to confess, over a celebratory bottle of Scotch, that he only went into the profession under the misapprehension that it would entitle him to wear a wig.)

Anyway, it was with the first glimmer of hope that I arrived at the familiar environs of the Rand Supreme Court, Wim by my side, chain-mail clanking under his robe. I detected a brief hesitation when he entered the gladiatorial arena — Court 6A — and saw he was matched against the notorious Ishmael Semenya. Dynamite comes in small parcels and there are few with as much explosive potential, pound for pound and inch for inch, as Ishmael. Fortunately there are a limited number of inches to him.

There were tense moments. Winnie's team played their trump card early, producing an affidavit from Kaiser Matanzima announcing he had whipped up some muti guaranteed to make me her slave again. I nearly had a heart attack on the spot. Fortunately when details of the ghastly brew were disclosed — mashed up tadpole eyes with other ingredients too awful to mention — Judge Frikkie Eloff mumbled "it doesn't work", casting a furtive eye at his wife who was lurking on the press bench pretending to be a Penthouse Pet.

Advocate Semenya then announced that he would be producing a surprise witness who would reveal that the breakdown of the marriage had been engineered by the top secret security branch unit, Stratcom, in a diabolical plot involving Magnus Malan infiltrating Winnie's bed disguised as one Dali Mpofu. Frikkie refused to hear the witness, saying it sounded too disgusting to be relevant.

At this stage Winnie, clearly disgruntled with the course of the proceedings, announced to Semenya that he was fired and rose to her feet to address the court. This caused general consternation. Wim took up a defensive position behind his law books and Frikkie, pausing only to fish his dentures out of his water carafe, bolted for the door, shouting over his shoulder: "The decree is granted to the plaintiff."

Winnie left court swearing revenge the next day when the hearing resumed for argument on the financial settlement. But when we duly assembled she failed to appear. Frikkie hurriedly announced that I had won by default and could keep all my possessions, including my precious collection of Valentine cards.

We had to walk down the stairs; someone was screaming for help from the stuck lift with a voice that sounded uncannily like that of my ex-wife. I then noticed that Wim had grease stains on his hands and a wide grin on his face.

There is nothing like a professional.

Nelson

*I*t was disclosed in early April that an ambitious scheme was being hatched with the President's approval to build a monument to "freedom" — a gigantic representation of Mandela's hand, cast in bronze. *The sponsors of the scheme were a pair of Johannesburg businessmen, the Krok twins, who had made their fortune by selling skin-lightening creams to blacks brainwashed during the apartheid years into believing white was beautiful. The project was so unlikely that when the story was published it was widely dismissed as an April Fool's joke. The scheme was subsequently aborted by the embarrassed President.*

OFFICE OF THE PRESIDENT

April 10 1996

Dear Walter,

Thank you for your patience in not asking about The Hand. The whole thing was so embarrassing I have not wanted to talk about it. But it is time I unburdened myself and I know I can count on your discretion as well as your sympathetic ear.

It all started, as these things do, with a phone call. It was Pik Botha, whispering down the line that he had just had a tremendous idea — as well as a third bottle of witblitz — for a tax-deductible scheme which would enrich us all and gladden the hearts of the nation. He said he could not explain it on the telephone, because one never knew who was listening in and it would be just like the CIA to pinch the idea because they would do anything to get rid of the Statue of Liberty which they saw as a KGB plot to discredit them.

I was a little perplexed by this cryptic approach, but reluctantly agreed he should come around — putting down the phone to hurriedly shout for Parks to get the bottle of KWV that I won at a church tombola last year, as well as my cough mixture, and secure both in the presidential safe. I just had time to make sure that the womenfolk were safely locked away in the presidential bunker when there was a knock on the front door.

I opened it to find a furtive-looking Pik disguised as usual in a self-evidently false and moth-eaten moustache in the company of two vertically challenged persons whom he introduced to me as "the twins". He then led us hurriedly into my bathroom where he locked the doors, turned on all the taps and looked suspiciously into the toilet bowl before closing the lid and sitting himself down upon it.

With a solemn flourish he pulled several documents out of a briefcase he was carrying, as well as a pen, and by mime indicated that I had to sign them. They turned out to be sworn undertakings in terms of the Official Secrets Act that "nothing said in the confines of the said bathroom will ever be divulged to any nosy-parkers masquerading as 'the people'". These formalities complete he pulled a radio out of the briefcase, tuned it to the Voice of America, turned the volume to full blast and stood it on the shelf next to my spare dentures. He then announced he was going to let me into one of the great untold secrets of the liberation struggle.

These freedom fighters, he said — gesturing to the twins now crouching in the bathtub — were behind the most extraordinary, courageous and audacious guerrilla action of the liberation struggle. They had selflessly spent years and considerable sums of their very own money working to undermine apartheid by manufacturing and distributing creams designed to turn black people into white people, thereby making a mockery of the Population Registration Act, not to mention complicating the administration of the Immorality Act and undermining the Group Areas Act.

Although the creams had not worked as intended, the piebald effect they had created on the skins of millions of South Africans had resulted in a collective mental breakdown among members of the Race Classification Board which had brought home to FW de Klerk the impossibility of sustaining apartheid, leading to my release from prison and the arrival of liberty, democracy and the introduction of live sex circuses in downtown Johannesburg.

By this stage of Pik's speech I had lost sight of him in billowing clouds of steam from the hot water taps and could barely hear him, what with Bill Clinton on the radio yelling threats to nuke Liberia and loud squeaking from the twins who seemed in danger of drowning in the bathtub. But he was mumbling on about the twins inadvertently making large sums of money out of their heroic actions and proposals to build a glorious monument to freedom and skin-lighteners and would I like a hand in it? By this time I was stumbling around in the steam, desperately fumbling for the bathroom door and shouting, "Yes, yes, anything, just get me out of here."

Well, you've seen the result. It was a nice touch to put it on Robben Island. But I can't help feeling that ships sailing into the fairest cape in the entire circumference of the globe are going to be a mite puzzled by the sight of the world's largest cast bronze giving them the two's-up.

Yours,
Nelson

S outh Africa was treated to high drama as a team of patriots attempted to plant the country's flag on the summit of Everest for the first time. Unfortunately feuding broke out at an early stage of the expedition, between journalists from the Johannesburg Sunday Times — sponsors of the climb — and the leader of the expedition, Ian Woodall. At one stage Woodall reportedly threatened to murder the Sunday Times editor, Ken Owen. A Sunday Times reporter, Ken Vernon, complained he was refused a cup of tea when he was in extremis on the mountainside. The newspaper, after discovering Woodall was not a South African, withdrew from the expedition. Woodall and a South African woman, Cathy O'Dowd, did subsequently make it to the summit and back, but the team's photographer, Bruce Herrod, was tragically lost on the descent. The rights and wrongs of the expedition continue to be hotly debated wherever South African mountaineers gather.

OFFICE OF THE PRESIDENT

April 24 1996

Dear Walter,

Isn't it exciting! Have you been following it? It all goes to show that we South Africans have the ability to overcome all! Stand aside Hillary and Tenzing! The rainbow nation has conquered Everest! Admittedly it was only the base camp. But as my mother used to say: you have to start somewhere.

We had front-row seats, courtesy of Joe Nhlanhla and the National Intelligence Agency, who installed a ham radio set in my sitting room, cobbled together out of second-hand listening devices returned to them by George Fivaz. The reception was not very good, being constantly interrupted by howls and crackles and what sounded like George slurping at his soup. But with the help of our imaginations there was enough to conjure up the exciting scenes in those frozen wastes above Katmandu.

There was the heroism of Ken Owen, tottering up the slopes

hotly pursued by a Sherpani (the female variation of a Sherpa) jabbing at his rear-end with a syringe filled with cortisone in an attempt to keep his gout in check. His squeals live on in my memory. No sacrifice is too much for a true patriot. I cannot wait for his return; it will be a privilege to pin the Cross of Good Hope (Second Class with Crossed Alpenstocks) on whatever portion of his anatomy survives the frost-bite.

Then there was the intrepid adventurer, Ken Vernon. Has there ever been a more extraordinary explorer's tale: how he fell asleep in his tent and his breath created a personal snowstorm?! He awoke to find a snowman leering down at him. My heart went out to him as he bounded down the killer-glacier in his polka-dot pyjamas yipping: "The Yetis are coming, the Yetis are coming! ..."

But they were heroes all, from the two girls skipping their way across the ravines, to 70-year-old Ken Woodall staggering along with his peg-leg determined to be the first man with piles to reach the summit.

There were, of course, difficulties, but what human endeavour is without them? One could only sympathise with Ian Woodall when he collapsed with an attack of vertigo trying to mount his chauffeured yak at Katmandu International Airport. But he, too, showed the Dunkirk spirit. When immigration officers pointed out that the South African passport he had treasured for so long as a family heirloom was in fact an expired season ticket to the Finchley municipal swimming pool, he wept only briefly for those wasted years on the Angolan border putting his life on the line for the editors of the *Sunday Times*.

The highlight of the assault on Everest came, of course, with the Battle of the Base Camp. It was difficult to follow this epic struggle among the squawks, whines and static on the radio, but it seems to have been triggered by Vernon's failure to remember the code-word when he attempted to enter the premises with his news team to get their constitutionally guaranteed cup of tea.

It was a terrifying moment as we listened helplessly to him and Ken Owen desperately intoning "Jani Allen ... red mercury ... Pofadder ... Prince Valiant ..." to the sound of avalanches crashing around them. Finally Woodall's patience seemed to break and we heard blood-curdling shrieks as he tried to tear Ken's head off his shoulders and loud thunks as Kate Owen bashed the expedition leader over the head with her umbrella. We lost reception for a while amidst the crackles. It came back briefly, enabling us to hear Owen's voice hopelessly declaiming: "I'm just going out; I may be some time ..."

It was at that stage that I determined to intervene with a presidential message urging our boys to press on regardless for the sake of national pride and the RDP. Unfortunately it transpired that the NIA's ham radio was only for listening in; it had no transmission capability. So we were forced to send a fax to "Woodall, c/o Everest."

Hold on, there is a knock at the door as I write; maybe it is a message ...

Oh Walter! Those gallant heroes! It was, as I feared, a farewell fax of reply:

"Had we lived I should have a tale to tell of the hardihood, endurance and courage of my companions which would have stirred the heart of every South African. These rough notes and our dead bodies must tell the tale." It is signed, seemingly in his own blood: "Owen of Everest."

There is a postscript: "Please cancel my subscription to the *Sunday Times.*"

Yours with a heavy heart,
Nelson

T he "final" Constitution of the new South Africa was passed by
Parliament in May 1995 after much brinkmanship from the
National Party. The Nationalists eventually voted for the Bill,
but immediately withdrew from the coalition government in protest at
the ANC's refusal to compromise on more issues. There were excited cel-
ebrations, but they proved premature — the Constitution subsequently
being rejected by the Constitutional Court on the grounds it did not
comply with the principles agreed under the 1993 political settlement.
A revised document was however certified by the court in December
1996.

OFFICE OF THE PRESIDENT

May 15 1996

Dear Walter,

Two marriages over in as many months and I don't even have to
worry about maintenance payments! Actually it was easier breaking
up with FW than with Winnie.

Now where did I leave you last week? Ah yes; Frederick had just
been carried out of the *bosberaad* strapped to a stretcher and gibbering in what I assumed was Afrikaans, but which Joe Nhlanhla,
who gets around a bit, later assured me was Basque. Whatever it
was he was hurried by ambulance to a single-medium lunatic asy-
lum as is his constitutional right. An anxious night ensued.

You will appreciate the difficulty we faced as the hours ticked
by. We had until 12 noon the following day to pass the country's
final Constitution with Frederick's help, failing which Gatsha
Buthelezi as Minister of Home Affairs would be entitled to organise
a referendum with the consequences we saw in Eshowe during the
general election when 800 percent of the population voted for him
as emperor.

Frederick clearly needed immediate psychiatric attention. The
problem was getting the permission of his next of kin. Marike was

the obvious candidate. But ever since I winkled her out of Libertas
by a stratagem, she has been refusing to receive visitors, or take
telephone calls. She is holed up in the Deputy President's hovel on
the Groote Schuur estate with seven packs of pit bull terriers roaming the flower beds and Groote Tante Sarie Willemse manning a
machine-gun nest at the front gate. The code word required for
admission is changed every hour, as a result of which Frederick
himself has been unable to breach the defences for six months, on
one occasion being shot up on suspicion that he was me disguised
with the help of tippex.

Eventually, on the advice of Fink Haysom, it was decided that as
President I stood *in loco parentis* and was entitled to take decisions
on Frederick's behalf. The chief psychiatrist ruled out a lobotomy,
on the grounds that they rarely worked a second time, and we had to
fall back on shock treatment. And so we sat anxiously by the telephone through the night making half-hourly calls to the institution
for progress reports. It was difficult to figure out the progress that
was being made, what with all the crackling, screaming and shouting going on at the other end.

We were on tenterhooks when C-Day dawned. Grimly we gathered in the great chamber of Parliament and nervously watched the
clock edging forward. With just minutes to go to the deadline, the
doors burst open and Frederick strode in looking purposeful. The
only indications of his overnight ordeal were the few wisps of hair
on his head which were standing straight up, giving the impression
he was wearing a favoured, but much over-used, bottle brush.

You could have heard a guinea fowl's feather fall in the tense
silence as he took the podium. With a flourish he pulled out a handkerchief and blew his nose. It sounded like the Last Trump. Then,
carefully putting on his glasses upside down, he squeaked: "My
husband and I ..."

The rest of his speech, which will no doubt go down in the
annals of oratory with the Gettysburg Address, was drowned in
cheers as MPs stormed the podium. The last I saw of Frederick was
his feet kicking in the air as he disappeared squealing under a rainbow scrimmage of parliamentarians, black, pink, coloured, other-
coloured, Malay, honorary whites ... all anxious to slap him on the

127

back in spontaneous joy at the final passing of the old South Africa.

And thus our new nation was born. There was a momentary concern about the effect all the excitement had had on the financial markets, our currency plunging past the psychological barrier of two bottle tops to the rand. But Trevor Manuel persuaded us that it was all psychosomatic. So, to restore confidence, we staged a huge party at Fernwood and danced the night away, Trevor being photographed doing the salsa on a table top with a bottle balanced on his head which immediately restored the faith of foreign investors in our commitment to austerity, discipline, conservative banking practices and champagne.

I subsequently had a charming letter from Frederick which read simply: *"L'état, c'est moi."* Joe, who speaks Basque, says it translates loosely as "I resign". The man in a white coat who hand-delivered it said no reply was required.

What a graceful way to take one's bow from the centre stage! He will live on in all our memories.

Yours as ever,

Nelson

The withdrawal of the National Party from the Government of National Unity resulted in the retirement of a number of prominent figures from political life. Perhaps the most prominent was RF "Pik" Botha, the former Foreign Minister, who chose to say farewell to Parliament with a philosophical speech in which he spoke of the transience of life and compared the nation to a bushwillow tree which had flourished in his back garden in the face of all adversity.

OFFICE OF THE PRESIDENT

June 7 1996

Dear Walter,

How sad life can be. And never sadder than when old acquaintances, friends and, yea, even enemies — for they are all companions on our journey of life — fall by the roadside. Forgive the tear-stains on this page, but it was a moving moment in all our lives. The Great Heffalump has shuffled off on his final journey to that legendary place where the pachyderms gather to greet the Heavenly Maroela Berry amidst scenes of great conviviality. Pik Botha has departed our midst.

And what a farewell it was! His speech to Parliament last Friday will resound through time with the great philosophical statements of the past. Or it would have done if the Hansard writer had not been so busy weeping that she forgot to get it down. But no matter, it will live on in our memories.

I forget how he got to the point, but he explained that our wonderful nation was like a bushwillow tree he had had much trouble with in the back yard of his home in the Transvaal. This bushwillow tree had the annoying habit, he recounted, of growing leaves which hung on through the winter until the young shoots came out in the spring when they would fall to the ground, making a hell of a mess of the lawn.

Irritated beyond belief by this unnatural process, he had bought a chainsaw which shattered on the trunk of the bushwillow tree, demonstrating what ungrateful sods the Taiwanese were after all the favours he had done them in the past. Nothing daunted, he had persuaded an old friend in the air force to bomb the bushwillow tree with Agent Orange. But the said tree, by an act of arboreal stupidity, mistook the defoliant for fertiliser, as a result of which there were now a lot of little bushwillow trees cluttering up his lawn.

Waving his arms to encompass his fellow MPs, he cried brokenly that the tragic story of the bushwillow tree just went to show we were all "like insects which have escaped a squirt of insecticide". But there were more squirts in the offing, he muttered darkly.

Just the other night he had been swilling down the last of his precious 10-year-old maroela juice, made to an ancient formula passed on by his Great Aunt Matilda, when through the natural lens created by the bottom of the glass he had made an awesome discovery. Far off in the night sky he had spotted a heavenly body, which henceforth would be known to humanity as "Pik's comet", hurtling towards the earth. With the help of the five fingers which were not otherwise engaged with the maroela juice, he had made a lightning-fast calculation which had shown indubitably that the comet would hit earth in one month's time, dealing with any dinosaurs left loitering around since the last such encounter and, with a bit of luck, putting an end to the scourge of the bushwillow tree.

Was God lonely, he demanded of his open-mouthed audience, that he should have cluttered up the place with bushwillow trees? "Could it be that all of us are merely characters in God's dreams?" he shouted.

At this precise moment one of the parliamentary air-conditioners began to malfunction, members of the African Christian Democratic Party seemingly mistaking the ensuing drone for the snoring of the Almighty. To shouts of "Hosannah!" the familiarly bent figure of the Great Heffalump stalked through the doors of the debating chamber for the last time.

We shall never see his like again. Nor, hopefully, will the lovely bushwillow tree.

Yours,
Nelson

The Sarafina 2 scandal rumbled on with rumours of plans to stage a sequel to the anti-Aids play in an effort to recoup the losses incurred by the original production. Meanwhile another scandal had hit the government, with allegations that the Minister of Public Enterprise, Stella Sigcau, had once accepted a R50 000 bribe from the controversial casino king, Sol Kerzner. Sigcau denied it was a bribe, saying it was a donation to her daughter's education. She observed scornfully that, anyway, R50 000 did not go very far nowadays.

OFFICE OF THE PRESIDENT

June 12 1996

Dear Walter,

I do wish that the sage who advised Mrs Worthington not to put her daughter on the stage had also had a quiet word with Jacob Zuma where his 37th wife (or thereabouts) is concerned. There is nothing quite as much of a trial as a minister infected by the thespian bug.

I was alerted to the arrival of showbiz at the citadel of power this week by the appearance of a rash of theatrical posters plastered up on the Doric pillars of Union Buildings announcing the "world première of the smash hit musical *Sarafina 2½*".

Frankly I did not take much notice, being only an occasional theatre-goer. But the production was forcibly brought home to me when I arrived at our weekly Cabinet meeting to be met at the door by a young lady in a mini-skirt, brandishing a torch, who demanded my ticket.

When I confessed that I had not known that I required a ticket she looked furtively over her shoulder before whispering that she happened to have one spare at a knock-down price of R20. Fortunately I had a chequebook on me and, after suspiciously examining the signature, the young lady whipped a ticket out of her garter-belt.

The transaction completed I was ushered into the Cabinet room which, to my astonishment, had been turned into something of a playhouse — the Cabinet table, pushed up against one wall, doubling as the stage with what looked suspiciously like a pair of my monogrammed bedsheets strung across the front with the help of a fishing line. The auditorium was crowded by members of my Cabinet, excitedly guzzling popcorn and coke.

I had no sooner taken my seat than the lights dimmed and the bedsheets swung open to disclose what I at first mistook for an astronaut recently returned from outer space, but which turned out to be our Minister of Health, Nkosazana Zuma, disguised as an unmentionable part of the male anatomy clad in a giant condom.

A chorus line of scantily clad girls then tripped across the stage, giving pelvic thrusts and singing "Roll Me Over", before forming a circle around the said giant condom and rolling over, seemingly dead. The giant condom then sang the hauntingly beautiful aria "Why Doesn't This Thing Work?" It warbled the last words — "It must have had a hole in it" — to thunderous applause from the Cabinet, several of whom were openly weeping at the pathos of the moment which had seemingly struck a chord.

A group of Cuban doctors disguised as doctors in beards and white coats then rushed on from stage left and began banging the giant condom over the head with their stethoscopes shouting in broken English: "Naughty! Naughty! Naughty!" The giant condom shrivelled up on the spot and with a collective air of righteous indignation the gaggle of Cuban doctors scampered off, stage right, carrying the deceased maidens (or not, as the case may be).

A large figure in a tiara then came bounding in, stage left, which turned out to be our Minister of Public Enterprise, Stella Sigcau, playing a Thembu princess with relatives in high places. She sang the tragic aria "How High Are School Fees!", reaching a treble-C with the words "R50 000 doesn't go very far !" before plunging a stiletto between her breasts in apparent mortification at the size of her daughter's tuck-shop account.

She fell with all the nobility of a toppled redwood tree, the crash awakening the giant condom which scrambled to its feet and gazed down aghast at the expired Thembu princess. The condom then burst into a lament, "What's R50 000 against R14-million", before seizing the stiletto from its resting place and with a shriek of "Oh, happy dagger!" turned it upon itself. The thrust punctured the little bobble on the head of the giant condom, out of which over-size banknotes erupted geyser-like as the curtains crashed down to a standing ovation from the Cabinet.

I do hope we are not going to have a *Sarafina 3*.

Yours, as ever,

Nelson

OFFICE OF THE PRESIDENT

July 3 1996

Dear Walter,

There is great excitement in my household, and apparently else-where, about my pending visit to London to spend some time with Queen Elizabeth II. We get on quite well, the Queen and I. I think I wrote to you about the wonderful party we had on the royal yacht Britannia when she came out to South Africa on a package holiday last year — when Prince Philip fell into the grog barrel attempting to do a somersault in the course of a spirited rendition of the horn-pipe on the banquet table.

It transpires, however, that visits to Buckingham Palace are a different thing altogether from these holiday jaunts, being conduct-ed in a far more solemn manner. I have been receiving a string of po-faced gentlemen from the British High Commission who describe themselves as "Protocol" and insist on giving me long lectures on the things I can and cannot do, say, wear etc etc in the presence of Her Majesty.

Some of them are quite obvious. Do not speak until you are spo-ken to, unless you are a horse. No pinching the royal teaspoons. Don't ask for more at the dinner table and no jocular references to the marital affairs of Henry VIII, George III's arboreal friendships, or use of the term *"loskop"* in reference to Charles I.

Others are more obscure and point to the difficulties under which the monarchy labours in Britain nowadays. I was advised, for example, that I might encounter a strange character loitering around the front door of the palace with a tin mug. This was the Queen's eldest son who was perfectly harmless, although he sometimes laboured under the misapprehension that he was a tampax. It was as well, I was told, to slip any loose change I might have on my person into his tin mug as he was having some difficulty with alimony pay-ments at the moment and any such gestures of help would go down well with his mother.

I was also warned to beware of his estranged wife who was officially barred from the premises, but occasionally got past the front gate under the pretext that she had come to fix the telephones and then hid around the corridors, keeping a check on how much her estranged husband had gathered in his tin mug. The trick was to avoid eye contact with this young lady, because at the slightest encouragement I would find myself receiving telephone calls from a heavy breather and she would take to banging on my door at all times of the night and day, pressing presents upon me.

There might also be occasions at mealtimes when I felt my toes being nibbled under the dinner table, I was told. I should refrain from kicking out as this was unlikely to be a corgi, but rather the Duchess of York who occasionally slipped on to the premises disguised as a pekinese and believed that this was the manner in which consenting adults communicated.

Meals, I was advised, were particularly perilous where potential *faux pas* and acts of *lèse majesté* were concerned. It would become apparent, for example, that the English monarchy had an obsession with beef. Many of the staff who wore funny clothes were known as "beef-eaters". The royal menu was inevitably composed of items such as "beef ritz", "beef stroganoff", beef caramel" and "beef extract au lait". This was merely symbolic, however. It was regarded as "non-U" to remark on the fact that these dishes tasted of soya beans. Her Majesty, it was explained, was traumatised as a child by a German aunt who persuaded her that English cows were given to cannibalistic practices and she was now convinced that the troubles suffered by her family were all attributable to a local outbreak of Creutzfeldt-Jakob disease.

There have been furious arguments with "Protocol" about how I should dress at Buckingham Palace. They want me to wear leggings and hose. I, of course, favour my colourful shirts.

Parks has suggested that I compromise, by going disguised as a man in a white coat. I could then mingle with the crowd.

Yours as ever,
Your old cell-mate,
Nelson

PALACE OF VERSAILLES

July 17 1996

Dear Walter,

Well, it is all turning out to be an incredible success. Gigantic crowds, massed bands, cheering children presenting me with squashed beetles and half-gnawed toffee apples — even the corgis joined in the fun, savaging two suspicious-looking men wearing bear-skin hats whom they found loitering around the gates to the palace.

The Queen did worry me a little. She seemed a trifle down, walking with a slight hunch and clutching herself in an uncertain manner. At first I suspected she had been drinking too much rooibos tea — as you know, our producers have tried to improve its foul taste with flavouring of irradiated rat-droppings. But it transpired that she was trying to cover up the darns in her cardigan and the ladders in her stockings.

When she saw I had seen these sad marks of poverty she burst into tears and confessed an awful thing had happened to her. As is well known her eldest son, whose friendships with cabbages had raised some doubts about the future of the monarchy, had transferred his perverse attentions to a neighbour's rottweiler and has been insisting on a divorce so he could pursue his affections untrammelled by conscience. He was, she sniffled, her favourite if errant son and she had capitulated, selling the family silver and pawning the crown jewels to pay the huge divorce settlement. She was so destitute that she couldn't afford petrol for her Rolls Royce, she said — weeping afresh as we clambered into a horse cart for the trip down Pall Mall.

I endeavoured to comfort her, promising to see if I couldn't get her a South African passport which would enable me to slip her into the RDP. But just as she seemed to be recovering herself there was a tooting from behind and a skeletal princess waving gaily behind the wheel of a Mercedes sports car with a "Buy British" sticker on the bumper flashed past us, precipitating fresh paroxysms of grief from my hostess.

But otherwise the British leg of the tour went off very well, including a series of meetings with captains of industry, merchant bankers and other men of great wealth who enthusiastically promised to liquidate their assets and invest their all in the rainbow nation — the effect of which was to send the rand into a fresh nose-dive. As that Danish character put it: "There are more things in heaven and earth, Horatio, than are dreamt of in economics."

And so it was on to France where I had a fine reception with more cheering crowds, massed bands and cheering children presenting me with squashed snails and half-chewed frog's legs. After a brief business luncheon with Jacques Chirac, during which he attempted to sell me a collection of postcards of dubious taste as well as half a dozen second-hand nuclear bombs, we proceeded down the Champs-Elysées to the Place de la Concorde where there was a massive traffic jam caused by an attempt on the part of members of the armed forces to stage a military parade. Chirac explained it was all in celebration of an occasion in the 18th century when the French had great fun chopping each other's heads off, adding with a leer: *"Voilà,* we are all revolutionaries together, *n'est-ce pas?"*

The garlic, which is the staple food in this part of the world, does not seem to agree with me. I had a nightmare last night. Winnie was sitting on a chair in Church Square, in front of a blood-spattered guillotine, busily knitting a scarf for me. There was a loud rumbling and I looked up to see a tumbrel rolling towards us down Church Street. On the back was FW de Klerk looking pale and Marike leaping up and down, shouting: "Let them eat cake!"

I think we do these things better in South Africa.

Wish you were here,

Nelson

At the beginning of September Mandela confirmed long-running speculation that he had fallen in love again — with Graça Machel, the widow of the late Mozambican president, Samora Machel.

The existence of a Mandela doppelgänger mentioned in the following letter goes some way to explaining curious statements made by the President over the years, notably his appeal to the Judicial Service Committee to appoint the country's first black judge as Chief Justice — an appointment in his own gift.

OFFICE OF THE PRESIDENT

September 17 1996

Dear Walter,

Sorry to have been out of touch. I have been away, enjoying something of a honeymoon with the beautiful, bountiful and wondrous Graça.

I know that your eyebrows must have risen a little at that assertion (that I have been away, I mean, rather than the unquestionable wonders of Graça the Ineffable) — considering that you have seen me parading around the place for the last couple of weeks on television and so on. Perhaps it is time that I let you in on one of the great secrets of state. Promise not to tell anyone?

I have a *doppelgänger*, Walter. A double. That's right, a man who looks exactly like me! It is in fact common practice among heads of state to have teams of *doppelgängers*, masquerading as oneself. They are very useful when assassinations are being planned and are also a convenience when one wants to get away from the strains of office without the *hoi polloi* going on about presidential salaries and wastage of taxpayers' money.

Of course with 300-billion people around the world everyone has many doubles; it would be impossible for nature to avoid duplication from time to time. Unfortunately, when I came to power, the security services had some difficulty locating mine (something to do with the shape of my ears, I believe, a model which nature did apparently forswear at an early stage of production).

Eventually a candidate was located, however; a character identifying himself as "Fred", running a pie store in Papua New Guinea. He was duly persuaded, with offers of large sums of money, golden days with bikini girls on Clifton and so on, to settle in South Africa and do the right thing by me when bullets are flying.

Reliance on one *doppelgänger* has, however, caused some problems. It is easy enough, when one has a team, to prevent their developing delusions of grandeur by switching them around from time to time. But when you have only one double — particularly when that one is a former pie-store owner called Fred — a tendency towards presidential pretensions is perhaps inevitable.

In fact many of the so-called political blunders which have been attributed to me have been the work of Fred. Remember the occasion when I called for 14-year-olds to be given the vote on the grounds that they were old enough to fight for liberation? That was Fred. In fact he called for the franchise to be extended to four-year-olds, arguing that anyone old enough to get tummy gripe is old enough to vote. Fortunately the reporter interviewing him thought he had misheard.

Fred is also to blame for this embarrassing confrontation I'm having over the Chief Justice. He (Fred) was the idiot who wrote off to the Judicial Service Commission urging them to appoint Ismail Mahomed. When a puzzled reporter asked me (Fred that is) whether it wasn't his decision anyway, Fred began shouting that he had rights like any other citizen, before Parks managed to shut him up with several sharp kicks to the ankle.

Sometimes I wonder if Fred is worth the trouble. Particularly when I catch him winking at Graça.

If it were not for his ears I would be worried.

Yours,

Nelson (not Fred)

*I*n October it emerged that a group of black executives had met in secret to form an "Africanbond" aimed at securing and promoting black business interests. There were heated denials that the organisation was in any way comparable to the Broederbond.

OFFICE OF THE PRESIDENT

October 11 1996

Dear Walter,

I'm not sure whether I ought to be asking you this question. Maybe I should wait until I see you when we can have secret handshakes and make furtive signs to one another, not to mention exchanging the odd nod and wink. We are, after all, sworn to silence ... Oh, what the heck; I'm sure the postal services are to be trusted. So here goes: have you joined the Bantubond?

I'm sure you have. Isn't it exciting! And to think I nearly turned it down. When I found the invitation pushed under my bedroom door, advising me to be at the Voortrekker Monument at midnight on Saturday if I wanted to hear something to my "financial advantage", I thought it was just another of these Nigerian get-rich-quick schemes. You know, the kind Tokyo is always going on about — which leaves the victim desperately sniffing castor sugar through a rolled R10 note, with his house under a second mortgage and his wife and daughters swimming out to ships. But something about the invitation caught my attention. It had a certain air of authority. Possibly because it was signed in blood.

"Nothing ventured, nothing gained," I rationalised. So when the witching hour approached I kitted myself out in what the fashion industry calls "Madiba Smart" — incorporating a pair of bed-socks and a rainbow-nation nightcap thoughtfully knitted for me by Tante Kriel to keep out the cold night's air — and headed off for that celebrated monument which has stood so long as an inspiring symbol of the centuries-old struggle by the Afrikaner nation to secure jobs for the boys and a holiday home for FW de Klerk in De Hoop nature reserve.

Pondering the appropriateness of the Voortrekker Monument to all liberation struggles, I trudged my way up to this sacred place and came over a rise to be confronted by an extraordinary sight. Gathered under some trees was a chilling assembly of people wearing cowls and bedsheets in the manner of the Ku Klux Klan. Except these sheets were black, albeit plastered with sponsors' advertisements ... the Development Bank of Southern Africa ... Transnet ... SABC ... Worldwide Africa Investments ... Telkom ... New Age Beverages ... Herdbuoys ...

In a trice I was surrounded by these frightening figures, all giving muffled cries under their cowls ... "It's him!" ..."It's the President!" ... "Oh goodie, goodie!"..."Now we'll get on presidential delegations!" ... Then one voice, sounding suspiciously like my old friend Barney Pityana, took charge. In grave tones he began to recite: "Do you, Nelson, solemnly swear by the blood of this chicken (here he violently produced a Kentucky Fried Party Pack from under his bedsheet) in the name of the brotherhood to ensure black intellectuals and blacks in business can engage in the totality of South African life and begin to make their presence felt and to drive the process of transformation and not leave it up to other people ..."

The rest of the swearing-in passed like a dream. And then it was all over. As one they cried "Welcome Broeder!" — throwing off their cowls. Spellbound I gazed at those dear and familiar faces — Saki ... Zwelakhe ... Wiseman ... But could it be? Yes it was. Even under the running boot-polish, the moustache was unmistakable. Seeing my incredulity he shrugged philosophically.

"It was the only way out of a black hole, Broeder," said Pik.

Yours in secrecy,

Broeder Nelson

T *he US Secretary of State, Warren Christopher, visited South*
Africa in October. He was trying to persuade African leaders to
help create a US-funded peacekeeping force for the continent.
The scheme reportedly received short shrift from Mandela.

OFFICE OF THE PRESIDENT

October 18 1996

Dear Walter,

Another of the burdens of high office is meeting foreign dignitaries.
They rush into my office with an entourage of photographers, grab
my hand and pump it up and down grinning inanely at the cameras
before rushing out again. Frequently I do not even get as much as
an introduction.

Sometimes, of course, I have to go out to the airport, which does
not necessarily make much difference. This week, for example, I
had to rush out to greet the American Secretary of State,
~~Christopher Robin~~ Warren Christopher. There was great excitement
as he touched down, all our VIPs jostling for position on the apron
in the hopes of scrounging another invitation to Atlanta. The stairs
were pushed into place, the door swung open and this character who
looked alarmingly like a desiccated prune came tottering out.

He took one look at the assembly gathered expectantly below
and tottered back in. Shouts, screams and banging noises emerged
from within the aircraft before he emerged again, this time with two
determined-looking aides clutching each elbow. He shrugged them
off and, with an imperious wave, called out in a reedy voice: "How
happy I am to be here in Sarajevo at last!" A sharp kick on the
ankle from the aide on his left evinced a wince, followed by a look
of dawning comprehension. "Oh, the darkie problem!" he
exclaimed, taking a kick to the right ankle.

I stepped forward to greet him as he hobbled down the stairs.
"The bags are in the back," he said gruffly, before kneeling to kiss

the ground in the style of the Pope. Or at least that was what we thought he was doing. His close communion with the tarmac had lasted several minutes when it became apparent that he had fallen asleep. With grunts of exasperation his aides lifted him into the boot of a waiting limousine and he was whisked away to the quavering strains of *The Star Strangled Banger* from an assembled brass band.

We met again at a state banquet that evening. He had been shaking my hand and grinning inanely at the cameras for some time when he noticed me. His jaw dropped open and he snatched his hand away, exclaiming: "You again! I thought I gave you a tip!"

After hurried whispers in his right ear by one of his ever-present aides another look of dawning comprehension crossed his face: "Ha, ha, just joking, just joking, must be the sun," he cried, "sun-tan lotion hasn't reached these parts, eh?"

With that he threw one desiccated arm around my shoulder and drew me to one side. "Listen, fella, I've got a message from your old friend Bill," he murmured confidentially. "He says to tell you if you'd like to set up a peacekeeping force we'll supply you with all the weapons you need ... Well, no nukes for the moment, but if you play your cards right ... The point is for a small price you'll have plenty enough to blow away anyone who gets in the way of peace ... Well, we've got to charge you something damn it!! ... And you'll be able to wear as many medals and other gee-gaws as you want ..."

The message delivered he gave me a slap on the back and — with a murmured aside to an aide of "Not my fault; thought he'd have bones in his nose ..." — the world's policeman tottered off.

Yours,
Nelson

T
here was some confusion in November at a report in The Star
*suggesting that President Mandela had withdrawn support for
his deputy, Thabo Mbeki, as his successor.*

OFFICE OF THE PRESIDENT

November 12 1996

Dear Walter,

Life, I am beginning to realise, is intrinsically a battle between good
and evil. And for some of us the struggle is personified. Batman, for
instance, fights it out with the Joker. Sherlock Holmes gave his all
in mortal combat with Professor Moriarty. Fate, it seems, has landed
me with the Polish dwarf and illusionist called Jarusvalskei.

I think I have written to you about Jarusvalskei before, Walter.
For some time I nursed the suspicion that he was masquerading as
FW de Klerk. You will recall that fear was allayed by the National
Intelligence Agency after lengthy investigations and experiments
involving the use of a theodolite. I was wrong that time, but on this
occasion I am confident that I am right.

I am not sure when it first began to dawn on me that our Deputy
President might be Jarusvalskei in disguise. I probably had my first
inkling when Thabo stopped wearing his pipe. It is not widely
known, but Jarusvalskei is allergic to tobacco (Anton Rupert, among
others, has confided to me in the past the suspicion that the vile
calumnies spread about the linkage between tobacco on the one
hand and the attenuated life expectancy of cigarette-puffing laboratory mice on the other were the work of Jarusvalskei).

The conclusive evidence came last week, when Thabo
announced he was going to Germany on a mission to encourage
trade and investment. You will appreciate that ever since our patriotic youth starting trying to close the north-south trade gap by murdering senior executives of German multinational corporations,
trade missions to the Fatherland have become pointless. For Thabo

to have been ignorant of this implied he was either Rip van Winkle or a *doppelgänger*.

Marvelling at his disguise I nevertheless decided to wait until he had safely left our shores before denouncing him to all and sundry. The ideal opportunity came on Friday when I found myself being interviewed by the correspondents of the world's three most distinguished newspapers, the *New York Times,* the *Times* of London and the *Naboomspruit Clarion.* I was about to spill the beans to them when, to my astonishment, the glamorous correspondent of the *New York Times* blurted out: "Is your successor Thabo Mbeki?" She knew, Walter! She already knew!!

Mentally making a note never again to question the investigative talents of the media, I confessed that I did not know. They looked aghast, as well they ought. A little concerned that I should, perhaps, have consulted more widely before going public on the scandal, I hurriedly qualified my statement: "The ANC will have to decide, of course. We are a democratic organisation after all," I added sternly.

Well, you saw the headlines, Walter. "Mandela drops Mbeki bombshell," squawked *The Star.* My heart leapt when I read it. Thank heavens for my favourite guru and editor, Peter Sullivan; once again he had lived up to his personal credo — to "tell it like he thought it was".

Then I read the story underneath, with growing horror. "President Mandela said yesterday Thabo Mbeki was not his heir apparent." They'd got it wrong! I'd said my heir apparent was not Thabo Mbeki!!

Round One to Jarusvalskei. What am I going to do? A Polish dwarf is one heartbeat away from the presidency!

Yours in turmoil,

Nelson

1997

T*he repeated failure of the Angolan rebel leader, Jonas Savimbi, to turn up for summit meetings has contributed to the collapse of peace initiatives designed to bring a final end to hostilities in that troubled country. The Unita leader appeared to have done it again in January when he failed to make an appointment to meet Mandela at his holiday home in the Transkei — a meeting set up by Thabo Mbeki in a burst of behind-the-scenes diplomacy. The meeting did take place a day late, but appears to have been fruitless. At the same time a startling peace initiative emerged in troubled KwaZulu-Natal, with disclosures that the ANC in the province was proposing a local extension of national amnesties for political violence as a peace offering to Inkatha.*

OFFICE OF THE PRESIDENT

January 8 1997

Dear Walter,

"Getting away from it all" — what a misleading phrase that can be. I've been holed up here in Qunu for the festive period and "it all" has doggedly followed me.

Why I allowed myself to be bamboozled by the local chiefs into setting up my holiday and retirement home in the Transkei heaven only knows. I've told you before how some idiotic architect with a sentimental streak chose to model the house on the isolation unit I last occupied at Victor Verster Prison. Taken in conjunction with such memories as the antics of the mad axeman of Qunu on the occasion of my circumcision, this is the last place I feel like spinning out my golden years. Almost enough to make me postpone my retirement. That would start some weeping and wailing from Thabo. Hee hee... !

Thabo is largely responsible for the disruption of my holiday although he is not the only one. You would have thought this was an airport terminal, the way they come stomping through my front door.

Heading the stampede was Jacob Zuma yelling "peace in our time" and waving a piece of paper over his head which turned out to be a proclamation extending forever the amnesty cut-off date in KwaZulu-Natal — to placate Gatsha and his legions and persuade them that we had always recognised their inalienable right as a warrior people to massacre their fellow citizens in large numbers without fear of judicial consequence.

The telephone never stopped jangling with calls from that emigrant rugby player, Francois Pienaar, who appears to have adopted me as his favourite uncle and keeps calling from Britain to whine about the high price of sun-beds and the difficulties inherent in playing the game on skis.

But it is this fellow Savimbi who provoked most of the trouble and for that I have Thabo to thank. Our Deputy President (First Class) has been suffering some angst recently about his ability, or otherwise, to fill my size 11 shoes and has been trying to prove his mettle. Taking advantage of Alfred Nzo's near-terminal somnambulance he determined to score a foreign policy triumph in Angola.

In pursuit of this hare-brained scheme he spent the Christmas period in Luanda, hanging around street corners, buttonholing passers-by toting pearl-handled pistols and inquiring as to whether they were one Jonas Savimbi. After being forced to dance the can-can to fusillades fired by a series of indignant diamond agents — labouring under the misapprehension he was after their ill-gotten gains — he seems to have struck lucky, because I received a frantic call in Qunu from him at 6pm in the evening. Yipping with excitement he announced that Savimbi was dropping in to smoke the peace pipe and sign all manner of documents, understandings, guarantees, treaties, protocols and whatever else was needed to achieve peace in our time in Angola and secure the rest of the world's diamond fields for their rightful owners at 44 Main Street.

In a state of high excitement we rushed out into the road and formed a guard of honour with the Qunu massed choir in attendance clutching their music sheets ready to begin warbling "Hail to the chief" and "For he's a jolly good fellow".

I'm writing this by moonlight. It is 3am in the morning and the massed choir is collectively snoring under the hedgerows. There may be peace, but I'm nursing doubts whether it will be in our time.

Yours by moonlight,

Nelson

I*n January the South African Cabinet shocked its ostensible allies, including the US, with the announcement that it was planning to sell military equipment — notably gun-sights for battle tanks — to Syria. Thabo Mbeki, who pointed out that he had been away when the decision was made, promised to investigate.*

OFFICE OF THE PRESIDENT

January 15 1997

Dear Walter,

Home sweet home. I'm back in the nuclear bunker again. Most of the Cabinet is here, sitting morosely around the command table. Nzo is snoring away on a camp bed. Trevor Manuel is in the bathroom; pulling faces in front of the mirror. Even the prospect of nuclear war is not enough to get Trevor away from a mirror nowadays; he is practising frantically for the "charm offensive" he is scheduled to launch next month in an attempt to persuade the world he really is our Finance Minister and not an out-of-work plumber.

The one face missing from this distinguished if glum gathering is Thabo. Which is where the whole problem started. As you know, Walter, Thabo is now our "President-in-Waiting". Contrary to what some scurrilous newspapers would have the public believe, this is, constitutionally, a position quite distinct from "President-designate", or "President-elect". Ours is a democratic organisation and Thabo will have to submit himself to the popular will of the people at December's national convention along with everyone else, including out-of-work plumbers, who aspires to be head of state.

In the meantime Thabo is running the country. This has caused a degree of angst in the Cabinet which also likes to think it is running the country. Frankly even I like to have a stab from time to time at running the country, if only to justify my modest expense claims with regard to cheeseburgers with which I supplement the Spartan diet Ma Kriel imposes on me for the sake of the RDP.

So when the Cabinet assembled for its weekly meeting shortly before Xmas great excitement met an announcement by Jakes Gerwel that Thabo would not be able to make it, because he was busy settling various crises in other parts of the world. A babble of voices ensued as ministers enthusiastically debated what momentous decisions they could make in his absence.

Kader Asmal had the trump card: an offer he had received in his capacity as Minister of Waterworks to supply Syria with R3-billion worth of tank laser-targeting systems designed to put Israel down the plug-hole. To loud cheers the Cabinet immediately voted unanimously in favour of the deal.

You will have seen from the newspapers what happened next. Bill Clinton had apoplexy in the White House. Government spokesmen in Washington announced they had irrefutable intelligence that the laser gun-sights were to enable Syrian tanks to shoot down innocent jumbo jets over the Potomac. In terms of the Anti-Terrorism and effective Death Penalty Act this made the South African government — including presidents-in-waiting and/or -designate and/or -elect — liable to a lethal injection on next arrival at JFK.

I tried to defuse the crisis, with a phone call to President Clinton. But I had got no further than saying "Bill, we have to sort this out" than he began shouting: "I emphatically deny being in a Little Rock hotel bedroom on the night of September 12 1991 ..." and slammed the phone down.

So I had no alternative but to push the panic button which landed us all here, underneath Ammunition Hill. The question is whether we can survive a nuclear winter.

The explosion, when he finally arrives home and finds out what we have done, will no doubt spell the end of life as we know it. Thabo did so enjoy Disneyland.

Yours,
Nelson

*A*sked at a press conference about the presidential succession Mandela claimed he could not hear the question, because his hearing aid was faulty, an explanation which was met with laughter.

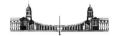

OFFICE OF THE PRESIDENT

January 22 1997

Dear Walter,

I know I have long complained to you about my inability to find peace and quiet, thanks to my onerous burdens and responsibilities as head of state. I write to give you the good news that I think I have discovered a solution.

When I left you last I think I was with the rest of the Cabinet, in the nuclear bunker underneath Ammunition Hill. You will recall that we were waiting for the earth-shaking explosions which were widely expected to accompany Thabo's return home from distant lands and his discovery that, in his absence, we had tried to flog various items of military equipment to Syria so that Hafez al-Assad could flush Israel down the plug-hole in furtherance of the Middle East peace process.

You can imagine the nervousness with which we took turns to monitor outside developments through the periscope which Modise has had installed in the roof of the bunker. A squeal of terror from Kader Asmal who was on guard duty at the time — and who carries responsibility for the whole debacle in the first place — alerted us to the approach of the President-Soon-To-Be-Ensconced (as, with notable humility, Thabo modestly allows his close friends to hail him).

We had all taken up defensive positions behind the few Spartan pieces of bric-à-brac which furnish the Cabinet's war-room when the doors burst open and, to our astonishment, there stood Thabo — unmistakable in his familiar built-up shoes, but with an unexpectedly wide grin ornamenting his face.

We emerged blinking into the sunlight to find ourselves surrounded by hordes of journalists excitedly shouting questions at me. At least I assume they were shouting questions, because at this particular moment I discovered that the battery for my hearing-aid had chosen to give up the struggle. I was, as a result, left trying desperately to decipher what they were saying from the movements of their mouths.

As I am unfamiliar with the art of lip-reading this resulted in some confusion which only became apparent when Parks was later able to inveigle a video recording out of the SABC from which I was able to reconstruct the ensuing press conference.

The first question was whether I was happy that South Africa was being hailed as the hero of the non-aligned movement for our stand on Syria. Under the misapprehension that I was being asked to comment on the third cricket test against India, I declared enthusiastically that it showed spin was not dead — an observation which had the questioner nodding sagely as he scribbled away in his notebook.

From the SABC video I was then seemingly asked whether I had a message for President Clinton. Assuming that they were once again prying into my relationship with the lovely Graça I replied stiffly that we were very much in love, but we had no immediate plans to marry, an answer which was met with a contemplative silence.

The exchanges continued in this vein for several minutes, culminating with a question as to whether I would be handing over power to Thabo this year. At this point I decided to give up the struggle to read their lips and come clean, offering my apologies and explaining that I couldn't hear a word they were saying, because my hearing-aid had broken down. This resulted in everyone falling about laughing and then giving me a standing ovation.

I've decided not to replace the battery.

Yours in quietude,

Nelson

T*he medical profession was startled by an announcement that South African researchers had found a cure for Aids. The three researchers had been given an unprecedented audience by the Cabinet to present their findings and parade patients who were said to have been cured by the treatment. The ethics committee of the Medical and Dental Council subsequently ordered a suspension of the clinical trials after it had been discovered that one of the ingredients of the cure was an industrial solvent which was known to cause cancer.*

OFFICE OF THE PRESIDENT

January 28 1997

Dear Walter,

How blessed our nation is with talent, imagination and, above all, inventiveness. I came face to face with the sheer genius of our people at last week's Cabinet meeting.

We were just about to start debating the whereabouts of Syria, a point which has caused violent altercations between our Defence Minister and Minister of Waterworks, when the third wife of Jacob Zuma leapt to her feet and announced that she had an important announcement to make. Ignoring the look of terror crossing most of her comrades' faces, she clapped her hands to be answered with a blare of trumpets. The doors swung open to admit two men and a woman in white coats with stethoscopes around their necks.

Dr Zuma excitedly explained that these were doctors and, she added, her voice rising to a triumphant squeak, they had together and in the name of the RDP invented the drug code-named "Brand X" which would cure the world of Aids!!!

As she made this astonishing announcement one of the three doctors clapped his hands. To the further sound of trumpets the doors swung open again and three more personages came bounding in. These, said Dr Zuma, her voice reaching a pitch previously left unexplored by operatic adventurers, were the guinea pigs!

We were then invited to prod and poke the guinea pigs — who asked not to be named, because of the shame it might visit upon their families — as they engaged in a variety of exercises. There were expostulations of amazement as it dawned on ministers that these fit and vibrant human beings, full of new-found vim, life and energy, had been snatched back from the very brink of the abyss.

I asked politely what sort of doses of Brand X they had been taking and was told scornfully by Dr Zuma that, due to bureaucratic delays on the part of the ethics committee of the Medical and Dental Council, they had not been able to take any as of yet.

At this point we broke for intermission, an attractive young usherette selling cold drinks and popcorn, the inflated prices for which were explained away by Dr Zuma on the grounds that she needed the funds to service the unauthorised loan she had raised with the European Union to finance her last pitched battle with Public Enemy No 1.

We then resumed proceedings with an account by the woman doctor of the extraordinary circumstances of the discovery. She recalled how she was lying in her bath when her plastic duck sprang a leak and as it sank to the bottom uttering piteous quacks the idea had hit her. Springing out the bath with a cry of "Eureka!" she had sprinted down the road, causing three heart attacks among 15 male geriatrics on board a passing bus heading for the All Men's Final of the Push-a-Ha'penny contest at the City Hall.

At this stage the doctor broke off her exciting tale, explaining they had been advised to withhold further disclosures pending investigations into the suspected properties of the wonder cure to wash whites whiter than white, a development which could revolutionise the race relations industry.

On a motion from Dr Zuma we immediately voted to divert all the money earmarked for Barney Pityana's Human Rights Commission to the good doctors and gave them a standing ovation as they bowed their way out.

Thus are the frontiers of science ever pushed forward.

I wonder if they can fix my hearing aid.

Nelson

Early in February there were protests from ANC MPs at the discovery that South Africa's base in Antarctica was painted in the colours of the old South African flag. At about the same time The Star *newspaper in Johannesburg announced, in a small report buried on an inside page, that it had uncovered a conspiracy to take over the country.*

OFFICE OF THE PRESIDENT

February 11 1997

Dear Walter,

What a week! It was my guru at *The Star* who has saved us — Peter Sullivan, as he is known to his creditors. Or Padraig O'Sullivan as he is believed to have renamed himself in tribute to the self-sacrifice of tens of thousands of South African newspaper readers who contributed so selflessly to the campaign for the return of Jackie Onassis's diamond ring to its rightful place on the finger of that great Irish lady, Mrs Tony "Begorrah" O'Reilly.

The signal flare went up from Padraig's secret headquarters at 47 Sauer Street last Wednesday. It would have gone unnoticed except by those trained in the Great Game: a small article off-handedly mentioning plans for a *coup d'état.* "Secret group wants to seize power by 2004."

I was alerted to it by our Intelligence supremo, Joe Nhlanhla, who came rushing into my office hyperventilating with the effort of holding true to his vows of silence.

He did not need to speak. One glance was enough. "A top secret destabilisation campaign is being waged by an élite group of 38 former and present political leaders, bankers, businessmen and some prominent right-wingers to gain economic power and take political control by the year 2004."

I pressed the red "Buthelezi button" built into my desk. The thunder of little feet resounded throughout Tuynhuys as the crisis

156

teams swung into action. I raced into the emergency operations room — an abandoned pantry which Tante Kriel reluctantly made available to us on condition we did not smear peanut butter on the walls.

Grabbing the red phone which puts me through to the planet's leaders I made my frantic appeals for help ... "Bill ... Boris ... Whatchamacallit ..."

Intelligence is the key to such crises and around me state-of-the-art computers — linked to the great machines maintained by the CIA in the Rocky Mountains and Mossad in the back of Mrs Plotnikov's Matzoh Balls Shop — rumbled and whirred, emitting clouds of steam. Across screens flashed Big Bird satellite photographs and encoded messages from heroic agents united in defence of democracy — dripping brown boot polish from the brow as they steer their sampans down the steamy Mekong and shivering in their moth-eaten Yeti disguises on the slopes of the Himalayas ...

A squawk from an analyst signalled a breakthrough. It was an aerial photograph by a hang-glider pilot who had lost his way on a mission over Sandy Bay, ending up over the South Pole. The quality of his Aunt Daphne's Instamatic was not the best, but the detail was unmistakable.

Masquerading as the South African Antarctic base — but betrayed by the brilliant blue, orange and white plexiglass out of which it was constructed — was the headquarters of the diabolical conspiracy. I pressed the mobilisation button. Sirens howled.

As I write Kasrils is at sea, rowing frantically southwards in a lifeboat cunningly disguised by cardboard cut-outs as a Spanish corvette. Our attack submarine, the *SAS Emily Hobhouse,* will be following as soon as we can unplug Joe Modise from the conning tower. We will fight them on the ice-floes, we will fight them ...

Regards,
Nelson (Supreme Commander)

In February South Africa's northern neighbour, Zimbabwe — under the homophobic rule of Robert Mugabe — suffered some embarrassment with courtroom allegations that its former president, Canaan Banana, had made a habit of raping his male aides while in office.

Simultaneously South Africa's tourist industry also suffered some embarrassment with the disclosure that the King of Sweden, Carl Gustav, and his Queen had been washed out of their bedroom in the country's premier hotel, the Mount Nelson, after a pipe burst. This happened in hotels all the time, said manager Luis Pinheiro.

OFFICE OF THE PRESIDENT

February 26 1997

Dear Walter,

If you take big paces you leave big spaces, the wise men of Burma say of ambition. But you will appreciate the frustration. We are, after all, Africa's superpower. Yet the only decisive foreign policy initiative we have taken is a refusal to play Nigeria at soccer — a dazzling stand on high principle which, unfortunately, we had to abandon to jeers and raspberries from the popular stands.

Concerned at our dwindling prestige on the continent, I this week called together those officials who make up the inner circle of my administration and charged them with the immediate achievement of a foreign policy triumph.

I must say they threw themselves at this task with great gusto and enthusiasm. The Great Lakes crisis was immediately identified as the target. Messengers equipped with the appropriate forked sticks were dispatched to the region, summoning key players to a summit in Cape Town and warning them to bring their swimming costumes and large bundles of dollar bills — the exigencies of the accommodation crisis in the Mother City necessitating their staying at the Mount Nelson Hotel which has recently taken to trying to drown its guests as well as fleecing them.

But the big question was how we were going to subvert our guests — subversion being, as you know, an integral part of the negotiating process. Here, again, the issue was tackled with energy. Spymaster Joe Nhlanhla — who has been bathing in glory following the disclosure that his glamorous agent code-named "Swart Gevaar" had seduced the entire National Party Cabinet into majority rule with the help of a garter belt and a vibrator — excitedly indicated by sign language that he would mount a new variation on the honey-trap which he had learnt from his American colleagues.

Not to be outdone, our fabled Ninja-man, Ronnie Kasrils, announced in an even greater state of excitement that, with promises of a double cheque and an introduction to Archbishop Tutu, he had recently secured the services of the world's most celebrated chemical weapons expert who could be expected to produce a variation of a Mickey Finn which would make all participants at the summit amenable to our foreign policy objectives.

As the poet said, even the best laid plans will go awry. It transpired that Joe had been reading a biography of J Edgar Hoover, a man whose resemblance to a pit bull terrier was made all the more alarming by his predilection for dressing up in a pink corset and stiletto heels when on duty. Joe was inspired by the lead given by the great FBI chief to fire the unfortunate Ms Swart Gevaar and replace her with a new agent code-named "Priscilla".

Ronnie, meanwhile, had been inveigled by his chemical weapons adviser — in a complex deal involving cut-price Hispanic corvettes — to invest heavily in a consignment of Spanish Fly which was only two years past its "sell-by" date. A furious squabble developed between Joe and Ronnie over which secret weapon would be brought to bear on the distinguished gathering of sub-Saharan heads of state. Finally Dullah Omar intervened and, in a judgment worthy of Solomon, had the Spanish Fly fed to Priscilla who was then unleashed on the summit.

I will not go into lurid detail. Suffice it to say the summit collapsed in a shambles. My abiding memory will be of Robert Mugabe racing through the rose-garden at Groote Schuur pursued by Priscilla — hairy chest peeping over lurex blouse, thighs bulging in a lycra mini-skirt above army boots — shrieking: "Help! He's gone bananas" — a phrase the origin of which has always puzzled me.

Yours,
Nelson